Our Brother In Black

His Freedom And His Future

Atticus G. Haygood, D.D.

President Of Emory College,
Oxford, Ga.

DEWARD
PUBLISHING COMPANY

Our Brother in Black: His Freedom and His Future

© 2009 by DeWard Publishing Company, Ltd.
P.O. Box 6259, Chillicothe, Ohio 45601
800.300.9778
www.dewardpublishing.com

Cover Design by Jonathan Hardin.

Printed in the United States of America.

ISBN: 978-0-9819703-5-6

Contents

FOREWORD

Originally published in 1881, and revised by the author in 1889, *Our Brother in Black: His Freedom and His Future* is Atticus G. Haygood's concise and insightful study of race relations in the post-bellum American South. Dr. Haygood, president of Emory College from 1875 to 1884, reflects Southern progressive intellectualism in the aftermath of the American Civil War and consequent Reconstruction. At the core of Haygood's writing and thinking is an unflinching belief that God's hand was in the events expanding African slavery to American shores, the cataclysmic Civil War—devastation Haygood witnessed firsthand as a Confederate chaplain—and the ill-fated, short-circuited efforts to usher former slaves ("freedmen") across the threshold to full citizenship. Central, too, is Haygood's resolution that men of faith, black as well as white, can share common rights and responsibilities within a single free society, working for its progress and defending its liberties.

As a gifted intellectual—indeed, Dr. Haygood led Emory College beginning at the age of 35—it was a natural extension of his reasoning that education was a key element in building a "New South." Originating in 1874 as the watchword of renowned Atlanta newspaperman Henry W. Grady, "New South" idealism underscored the South's need for industrial and social progress. As might be expected, Haygood's *Our Brother in Black* does not concern itself as much with industrialism as it does the educational growth that the author argues is absolutely vital as a path for societal development. A proponent of a strong liberal arts education, though not necessarily opposed to Booker T. Washington's vision of a vocational base from which the sons and daughters of freedmen could build their case for full citizenship, Haygood's argument that an educated citizenry is the strongest bulwark for a democratic republic has antecedents stretching back to the Founding Fathers. While Washington's Tuskegee Institute—its founding in 1881 fitting neatly into Haygood's historical context—was largely the vision of one man believing his own race needed to "cast down (their) bucket" where they were, Emory College's young president viewed the matter of education as one of national, not regional, import.

Since the Civil War had yielded a consequence that the martyred Abraham Lincoln characterized in his brilliant second inaugural as both "fundamental and astounding"—a social, political and economic upheaval wrought by emancipation and a final Union victory cementing abolition—Dr. Haygood reasoned that the North as well as the South had a shared responsibility to educate freedmen, and by doing so, prepare them for the role of citizen which had been thrust upon them. Haygood's careful, sometimes sharp, argumentation for a progressive education offered to all Southerners—white as well as black—was echoed in later years by other progressive reformers, but perhaps never better made than in the following pages.

In twenty-first century America, most liberal academics and quasi-intellectuals might dismiss Atticus G. Haygood as, at best, a paternalistic educator covering his latent bigotry with idealistic calls for racial understanding pinned to Christian apologetics. Yet, a view of Haygood within his historical context gives a truer and fairer picture. In a Southern society becoming politically dominated by those like U.S. Senator James Eustis of Louisiana—whose parochial and racist stands Haygood takes his rhetorical sword to in the last three chapters of this text—Haygood was considered at least a Southern moderate. Though never explicitly calling for social equality in this work, Haygood nonetheless demands the best that our God requires of us: to respect one another without regard to race; to be truly brothers in Christ. In an America that, soon after the revision of this work, formally sanctioned "separate but equal" as a consequence of *Plessy v. Ferguson* (1896) and had already largely isolated Southern blacks from the voting box, Haygood's brave contention that education could create a framework for a politically biracial South was remarkable.

It is fitting that Atticus Haygood passed from this life in 1896. The type of Southern society he had championed—one built on both unchanging spiritual principles, as well as secular principles outlining democratic government by individual educated citizens of a republic—was being twisted into one trumpeting white supremacy within a set of near-sighted, dissatisfied Southern states. Even today, though voting rights were secured for all and racial equality mandated more than forty years ago, Haygood's fundamental quest remains: as His disciples, we seek to better serve our Lord daily, as well as our brothers of every color.

Brian Lewis Crispell, Ph.D.
Dean of Students | Professor of History
Florida College | Temple Terrace, Fla.

PREFACE TO THE 1889 EDITION

In bringing out a new edition of *Our Brother in Black* I have added three chapters, beginning with a "Reply to Senator Eustis," Chapter 19. The added chapters indicate the trend of thought in 1889.

Atticus G. Haygood
May 10, 1889

NEW PREFACE

Our Brother in Black: His Freedom and His Future. The book was first published in August 1881—a little more than a decade following the War Between the States—when even the concept of decent and equal treatment of the African-American was in sharp contrast with the predominant sentiment in the South. An educational system was essentially non-existent for either race. As the title suggests, Haygood's racial philosophy draws its historical meaning within the context of his deeply held Christian values that stressed the brotherhood of all members of the human race in Jesus Christ. The moral emphasis for this work comes directly from the Bible. He said, "Our obligation to help the Negro in his social and religious development does not grow out of 'our party,' or 'our Church,' but out of our common relation to Christ Jesus, our elder brother, and to our God, our Father." This drove the author's racial liberalism and moral purpose. This legacy—his insistence that the basis tenets of Christianity demanded modification of existing patterns of race relations—helped sustain future southern liberals in their campaign for liberty and justice for all.[1]

Atticus G. Haygood's *Our Brother in Black* caused much consternation in the South, published a year following his 1880 Thanksgiving Day epoch sermon entitled *The New South: Gratitude, Amendment, and Hope.* He was called "Nigger Bishop," and "Nigger College President," and, for several months, he was not invited to fill a Southern pulpit. This reaction was not unanticipated and the author was under no illusions. In remarks to a friend, Rev. Luke Johnson, Dr. Haygood wrote:

[1]John B. Boles, *Masters & Slaves in the House of the Lord* (Louisville: University of Kentucky Press, 1998), 171.

Battles are short and fierce with me. I am not superstitious, but on my knees I seemed to see the devil himself across my desk suggesting that if I took up this work I would be ostracized, the college over which I presided would be ruined, and the people would turn pen and tongue against me. I commanded... *"Go back to hell where you came from, for I will do it, God helping me."*

On the night that he finished his book, he wrote a friend, Rev. Eugene R. Hendrix, reflecting on the New South sermon, the present, and the future. He wrote:

Following the Thanksgiving sermon, I received scores of letters—nearly all from the North—not a line from any so-called *leaders* of our Church—anywhere—except you. What is to become of us! It nearly breaks my heart to see men so blind and deaf—to their age—they stand serenely—winking at each other and back at 1844—while the very ground under their feet is going down—*Fatuity*.[2] In God's name—I cut loose from deaf and blind and dead men. What torments me most is a few see and are afraid.

Be sure: I will press straight on. I am to preach in Atlanta, Sunday, on the Christian Citizen. I will tell you a secret—I have *just,* tonight, finished a 250 or 300 page book *[Our Brother in Black]*—discussing squarely & fairly the Negro in the South. It will be published right away. Don't mention it yet. My reason for silence now is that it might get back here and I don't want people to bother me with questions—they will have their hands full when it comes out.

Shortly following publication of *Our Brother in Black*, the leadership of the Methodist Episcopal Church, South did indeed adopt his stand on race relations, and elected Dr. Haygood Bishop in 1882. However, in a nearly unprecedented move, he declined ordination in order to complete his work of rebuilding Emory College following the War, and concurrently to lead a newly established philanthropy that was to help fund what are now known as the Historically Black Colleges and Universities (HBCU). Following publication of his popular *The Man of Gali-*

---

[2] A lack of intelligence or thought combined with complacency.

lee in 1889 and an updated edition of *Our Brother in Black*, also in 1889, he was elected Bishop a second time in 1890. This time he accepted the Episcope.

This history is in itself a fascinating read. Yet *Our Brother in Black* also shows how one individual can influence society for good while at the same time putting the dimension of time into perspective with regard to major undertakings to help those involved in such tasks avoid being too discouraged.

A United States election in which an African-American could be elected President of the United States may not have even been dreamt by Haygood when he formally launched his campaign for equality in 1880, aimed at the acceptance of all peoples as equal. In Haygood's view humanity was a single race.[3] Indeed, we have journeyed far since Haygood launched his transformative work in the late nineteenth Century; however, in the words of *Time of Grace* Televangelist Pastor Mark Jeske,[4] "the work of Haygood, Martin Luther King and other civil rights teachers and leaders is far from done. It may be that racism is just as much a core sin as lying and stealing and can never be eradicated from the human heart. Like all other sins, it needs forgiveness by God's pure grace, a change of mind and heart, and new learned behaviors in Christ." Dr. Jeske has served a congregation in the heart of Milwaukee's inner city for three decades and is one of thousands who are continuing Haygood's struggle today.

Our Brother in Black has been cited as the first significant example of white racial dissent after Reconstruction, in which Haygood applied the teachings of Jesus Christ to race relations—in today's vernacular—called the social gospel. Haygood used his authority as president of Emory College (now Emory University), and a leading Methodist minister to exhort the South to treat the African-American more charitably. He explained that true Christianity demanded changes in the existing pattern of black-white

[3]Joel Williams, *In Rage for Order: Black-White Relations in the American South Since Emancipation* (New York: Oxford University Press, 1886), 74.

[4]Mark Jeske, personal correspondence to William Shaker, July 14, 2009

relations in the South, and denounced perpetrators of racial violence as un-Christian. Most important was his prediction that efforts to keep black people poor and illiterate would in the long run drag their white neighbors down, saying, "It would be kinder, and more prudent, to provide former slaves with a day's work than a day's rations, there was no way out of providing one or the other. If society 'will not build schoolhouses and churches,' it must build jails. Thus reason and justice would get their grim revenge." Haygood was indeed a lonely voice even among his progressive white contemporaries who supported industrial education and the franchise, but who believed that the African-American would always exist in a subservient condition. Haygood envisioned an open and limitless future for blacks. Industrial education was the beginning, but it was not the end as far African-American possibilities. He was thus a dissenter from the New South realism that consigned southern blacks forever to political subservience, rather envisioning a different kind of racial pattern at some time in the future. His work—indeed his personal funding—to establish Paine Institute, which he described as an Emory in Ebony (now Paine College), was just one of his tangible commitments to new possibilities for blacks.

Our Brother in Black is an extended account and exploration of the role of freed slaves in the days of Southern Reconstruction. Their numbers and their characteristics, including their poverty, lack of education, and perceived moral shortcomings are described. In its pages one gets a feel for what southern people thought just after the Civil War.

Haygood maintained that if white people and black people wish to know how to treat each other in all the relations of life, they need to study the Bible:

> Take for example the business relations of life, the old question of capital and labor, of service and wages. For the settlement of all questions that grow out of these relations the laws laid down and the principles taught in the Bible, are worth all the "political economies" in the world. They apply to all races and conditions of men, in all countries and in all times. They are as needful

and useful in New England factories as on Southern plantations. Free Negroes are not the only underlings in the world; Negro servants are not the only hirelings. There are thousands of factory operatives, day laborers, domestic servants, mechanics, sewing women, clerks, apprentices, and such like, whose cry for justice against oppression goes up to heaven by day and by night. "The wrath of God is come upon the children of disobedience." Let us here recall some of these half-forgotten laws; they must do us all good. I know they are needed in the South; I am persuaded that they are needed wherever there are masters and servants.

Haygood argued that the South was the best place for African-Americans to live—for both whites and blacks—discrediting a popular campaign of the time that advocated sending all blacks back to Africa. He said that since "six millions of negroes" were in the south "to stay," and that since slavery had left the freedmen as unprepared for citizenship as a burned house would be for giving shelter, all Americans needed to be concerned about the education and financial support required to help the "Negro be a neighbor."

Haygood addressed emancipation, going into considerable detail about Abraham Lincoln and the motives behind the Proclamation. Throughout this process, the author focused on how best to move forward now that the slaves have been freed. He went out of his way to condemn the animosity and anger that existed between North and South on the race issue and examined how to prepare freed slaves for *full* participation in the community—not, as Haygood was careful to point out, simply for voting. To that end, he described efforts needed for educating African-Americans, including missionary work and black colleges, which he had a major role in establishing and structuring. In *Our Brother in Black,* he pondered potential new issues of race relations. In looking ahead to the year 1991 he wrote,

> I apprehend the difficulty of the subject taken in hand in these pages. The historian who may write of our times *a century hence* may offend—such is the sensitiveness and pertinacity of prejudice—some of the descendants of those who are now concerned

in such a discussion. But this he can do, endeavor faithfully to state facts as they may then appear to him. He will have many advantages over any writer of the present time.

Much smoke will have cleared away, and with it much heat and prejudice. Questions now in dispute will have been finally, and, let us hope, happily settled; experiments now only in process will have been ended. The historian, in forming his judgments upon our times, will have the benefit of results. If we could only foresee, and in a clear light, what will be very plain to him, we would understand not only our duties but also each other much better than we do now. (emphasis added)

Haygood's contemporaries described him as a generation ahead of his time. As we look back more than 130 years after *Our Brother in Black* was first published, it is clear that the book is progressive on numerous points. Yet if written today, it could be labeled racist. To a large extent, this fact might be attributed to Haygood's pragmatic insistence on accomplishment, as described in the 1889 Andover Review that depicted Dr. Haygood as a practical reformer, "one who enjoyed the great advantage of being far enough in advance of the people who he sought to persuade to be a good leader for them, yet keeping within their sight and where they could easily follow him." Although advocating separate schools for the races would be considered racist today, Haygood believed that insistence on an integrated education for the recently freed slaves would result in no education at all, thinking that the southern society of his time would find it impossible to educate the black man in integrated schools.

In 1893, two years prior to the Bishop passing, when the family returned to Georgia, Haygood understood that the fragile momentum of the revived mission to blacks that he had achieved in the 1880s had been lost. The current was running swiftly in the opposite direction. Haygood had assumed that the Fifteenth Amendment to the U.S. Constitution would not be violated. Writing prior to systematic "legal" disfranchisement, Haygood based a fundamental premise on the fact that since the Black man could vote, it was important that he be educated.[5] "Woe to the land where those who hold the balance of power are ignorant. The tremendous engine of political power, the ballot, must be in hands that know what they are doing." African-Americans were an absolute majority of the population in Mississippi, Louisiana and South Carolina, and represented over 40 percent of the population in four other former Confederate states. Haygood had every reason to believe that his premise was a solid one, since the Fifteenth Amendment to the United States Constitution was ratified in 1870 to protect the suffrage of freedmen after the Civil War, and it prevented any state from denying the right to vote to any citizen on account of his race.

Unfortunately Haygood's audience concluded from the same premise that the most pragmatic solution was simply to deprive the African-Americans of the ballot, accomplishing this disenfranchisement by entrenching "legal techniques" in their constitutions. Southern Democratic legislators created new constitutions with provisions for voter registration that effectively completed disfranchisement of most African-Americans and many poor whites. They created a variety of barriers, including requirements for poll taxes, residency requirements, rule variations, literacy and understanding tests, which achieved power through selective application against minorities, or were particularly hard for the poor to fulfill. Direct disenfranchisement and the attempts to use federal law to prevent disenfranchisement was to continue through 1965, when the Voting Rights Act was passed.

Ironically, Haygood's morally persuasive oratory would be used by President Lyndon Johnson as he defined civil rights as a moral issue in his campaign to pass the Voting Rights Act, which was a watershed in twentieth century political history.[6] In the second week of May 1964, President Lyndon B. Johnson electrified the nation by stumping Georgia on behalf of civil rights legisla-

---

[5]David L. Chappell, *Inside Agitators: White Southerners in the Civil Rights Movement* (Baltimore: The Johns Hopkins University Press, 1996), 5.

[6]Randall B. Woods, *LBJ: Architect of American Ambition* (Cambridge: Harvard University Press, 2007) 476.

tion. Speaking to the Georgia Legislature on May 8, 1964 the President quoted Haygood, who in 1880 had declared: "We in the south have no divine call to stand eternal guard by the grave of dead issues."

Haygood had always believed that resolving the race issue was a moral imperative, and he was not one to lose faith. However, Haygood never thought of the race issue as simplistic, believing it would become even more complex with time. In 1895, several months before his death, he wrote an article for *The Methodist Review* that would prove prophetic: "Our chief trouble with us (in resolving the Negro issue), as in all things, is this: we are in a great hurry about everything. But God is not in haste about anything. Time, faith, and labor, were the tools of progress, but progress would be slow."[7]

Resting his faith in the educational missionary movement that set in before the war was over; Haygood felt that immediate improvement must come from the South, there being patriotic, Christian people necessary for progress. However, he warned: "The North and the East were hobbled. With socialism, communism, and infidelities that curse these sections, they are not fitted to solve this (the Negro dilemma)."

He lamented the loss of hope by those who had been engaged in the education of the Southern Negro:

> They expected too much, and expected it too soon. They forgot history; else idealized the Negro. Many did idealize him, and did him infinite harm at the beginning—telling him much more of his rights than his duties. Alas for them! When the actual Negro did not measure up to their romantic dreams of him—an angel in ebony—hope died within them.

Haygood concluded with a prophetic projection to the year 1965:

> Those who are seeking the Negro's good, deal with at least three generations—the people set free, their children, and their

---

[7]Atticus G. Haygood, *The Methodist Review*, September-October 1895.

grandchildren. Our great-grandchildren, comparing 1865 and 1965, will rejoice, and glorify the Lord God and Father of us all. They will also help to build monuments to the heroic men and women whom their grandparents ostracized. Among and by those monuments half a dozen of our people and time will be remembered.

Bishop Holsey, the best known Bishop of the Colored Methodist Episcopal Church, was a founder of Paine College along with Haygood. Almost two decades after *Our Brother in Black* was first published, Haygood Hall was erected at Paine College in 1898. On that occasion, Holsey, a man who grew up a slave delivered these remarks about Haygood, the son of a slave owner, expressing the high esteem in which Haygood was held by the black community:

The new building that is now in process of erection at Paine Institute is to be called "The Haygood Memorial Hall," as a monument to that great man, who stood for so many years as a wall of brass in the defense of the Negro race in this country. In him, the Negro race had its strongest, its broadest, its truest, and its most eloquent and sincere friend. He was our Martin Luther, who with pen and voice, and with the deepest flow of soul, stood at the foot of the cross, and amid the declining decades of the dying century wrote his theses and nailed them upon the door of public opinion, and changed the tide of public sentiment in this country in behalf of the Negro race. He is not dead. He has only ascended to the city beyond the stars of God, while his thundering theses, so ably advocated, are ringing through the decades and over the surging waves of the expanding civilization, appealing to the considerate judgment, the patience and Christian charity of the Christian people of this country. Negroes should build a monument of steel to his precious memory higher than the Eifel Tower covered with gold and tipped with diamonds.[8]

This DeWard edition of *Our Brother in Black* and the Interna-

---

[8]Bishop L. H. Holsey, *Autobiography*, Electronic Edition (Chapel Hill: University of North Carolina, 1999), 193.

tional Platform Association posthumous presentation to of the Silver Bowl for a Lifetime Achievement in Education to Bishop Haygood might be considered part of that tower Bishop Holsey described.

William Haygood Shaker
Great-grandson of Bishop Atticus Haygood
Author of the forthcoming book, *Atticus G. Haygood: At the Crossroads of Change*

1

SIX MILLIONS OF NEGROES

The last census shows that there are nearly six millions of negroes in that part of the United States that is known as "The South." Comparatively speaking, there are few of them in the other sections of the Union—not enough to make an exigent question in labor, society, or politics. In the South the case is very different; the negroes are about one third of the whole population; in some States nearly one half. Thus, in Georgia, according to the census of 1880, the total population is 1,538,983; the colored people number 724,765. In some of the States they are in the majority.

The great majority of the colored people in the Southern States are pure-blood Africans, though many lighter skins among them show the mixture of races. The white blood betrays itself. This explains the hasty conclusions of some observers, traveling through the South. They think that there are very large numbers of mulattoes. They are mistaken, and not unnaturally. A score of black children are passed unnoticed; one mulatto is observed. In a country peopled with only one race there might be as many children born out of wedlock as there are mulattoes in any one of the Southern States, but there would be no evidence to the eye. But where white and black are blended the yellow skin advertises the origin of its owner.

As there are some prevalent misconceptions on this subject, one other remark may be allowed at this point; in the South the half-breeds are generally found in towns and cities, and from towns and cities most tourists derive their impressions of a country. But the great mass of the Southern population is rural. Of the entire Southern population hardly one million are in the cities.

When this whole subject, with its history and conditions, is well and fairly considered, and with the passionless attention that is bestowed upon any table of mere statistics, it will be concluded, I think, that there is but one other such case in history of a race living for generations within another race and yet keeping its blood so pure. The Jews alone can match this unique fact. Let it be observed that I am not speaking of the moralities implied in these remarkable parallels, but only of the fact of mixed bloods. The Americanized-Africans increase rapidly. They numbered about seven hundred thousand at the close of the war for independence. They have multiplied more than eight times in a little less than a century. How many will they be in the year 1991?

I apprehend the difficulty of the subject taken in hand in these pages. The historian who may write of our times a century hence may offend—such is the sensitiveness and pertinacity of prejudice—some of the descendants of those who are now concerned in such a discussion. But this he can do, endeavor faithfully to state *facts* as they may then appear to him. He will have many advantages over any writer of the present time. Much smoke will have cleared away, and with it much heat and prejudice. Questions now in dispute will have been finally, and, let us hope, happily settled; experiments now only in process will have been ended. The historian, in forming his judgments upon our times, will have the benefit of results. If we could only foresee, and in a clear light, what will be very plain to him, we would understand not only our duties but each other much better than we do now. Lord Bacon dedicated his history of Henry VII. to Charles, then Prince of Wales, and apologized for any defect in the picture in these words: "I have not flattered him, but took him to life as well as I could, sitting so far off, and having no better light." But this advantage he had, he did not sit too neat, and the light he had was without heat. An artist may sit too near his subject, and the light may be so intense or so crossed as to blind or confuse him. This is peculiarly true of those who, in a long and fierce conflict, have felt either the exultations of victory or the humiliations of defeat.

2

SOME CHARACTERISTICS

Most of these six millions of Africans are very poor. Fifteen years ago they had nothing but their trained muscle and their hope. Of multitudes of them this ought to be added—their faith in God.

During these fifteen years, which many of them have spent in trying to find their reckoning on a wide and unknown sea, most of them have had a sharp struggle for existence. A very few have shown good capacity for business and have accumulated handsome properties. A larger number have built themselves humble houses that are their own, and a few have got some foot-hold in the land, and are the owners of small farms. Most of them depend for subsistence solely on their labor. A very great majority of the whole number are in the rural districts at work as hired laborers, or as tenants, upon contracts renewable at the beginning of each year.

The fact that the great body of them are on the plantations and farms gives them one marked advantage over certain laboring classes of some States and countries—they are not subject to "lock-outs," nor are they liable to be thrown out of employment by "suspensions" or by "panics"; for agriculture does not suspend. They are beginning to appear upon the tax books as land owners. Thus, in Georgia, according to the "Report of the Comptroller-general" for 1880, the colored people own of "improved lands," 586,664 acres. The white people own 29,823,581 acres of "improved lands." That is, of the farming lands in Georgia the negroes own a little less than one acre in every fifty. All things considered, this is a very creditable showing for them. It may be doubted whether the average is quite so high in other Southern States.

With few exceptions the best lands are owned by the white people. It is easy to explain this. First, the whites have, as a rule, been reluctant to sell their lands to anybody. They cling to the land; it is an instinct. They have been doubly reluctant to sell lands to negroes; not because they have felt unkindly to them, but chiefly because they have been afraid that negro land owners would frighten immigrants from the South. Whether this fear is well grounded may be doubted. Some, it may be, have not wished to see the negroes land owners, from a vague prejudice, or a vague fear. This, I think, is clear; the negroes who own land in Georgia are more satisfactory as citizens and neighbors than those who do not. This is undoubtedly true of my negro neighbors.

The majority of the negroes live in small and, generally speaking, very uncomfortable and ill-furnished cabins. They have few comforts. But this gives them comparatively little trouble, for they live very plainly, and most of them have enough to eat, and, in winter, wood enough to keep warm. Most of them will spend their last dime for food or fuel; if it come to the pinch, some of them will get it elsewise, as will some white men. A fence rarely survives a cold winter if it be close to a settlement of negroes. The average negro will burn his own fence without hesitation. The necessity generally arises through his habit of putting off till tomorrow what he is not obliged to do to-day. Many of them are much like the improvident white man whose roof was out of repair. His explanation was: "It don't leak in dry weather, and I wont patch any man's roof in the rain." I have a negro neighbor who has burned his own fence and part of mine for four winters past. Next spring we will make a new fence. It is left to the reader's ingenuity to find out my reason for waiting till warm weather.

Nearly all of them are field-hands and common laborers; few of them are skilled workmen; the best mechanics among them "learned their trades" before the war. Free negroes and Southern white boys are alike at least in this—they are impatient of apprenticeship. This is one reason why the South is behind in the mechanic arts.

As a class the negroes in the South are not systematic in their plans and labors. They are not thrifty, or frugal, or economical. Few of them know how to "lay by for a rainy day." When they were slaves they never thought of such things; when sick, or old, or worn out, they were taken care of better than any class of superannuated laborers in the world. The exceptions to this statement were few. No railroad, or mining company, or great manufactory, can match the care the "old masters" took of their disabled or worn-out servants. And thousands of the old servants still look to their former masters for help, and receive it. The old customs made it unnecessary for the negro to provide for sickness or old age. Very naturally, therefore, the habit of forecasting has not been largely acquired among them. They spend their money freely while it lasts, much as children do. Instance, a colored man, who lives near me and who has no income but his wages as a common laborer, recently gave seven dollars for a flashily bound family Bible, being overcome by the arrangement at the back of it for receiving the family photographs.

Their weaknesses are perhaps partly in their blood; they may well be more in their antecedents. (Some of these "antecedents," it may be remarked, antedate their coming to America.) But, poor as they all are, and thriftless as most of them are, they are improving in their condition. The tax books show that they are beginning to produce a little more than they consume. They live better, dress better, have better furniture, than they had ten years ago.

Some things I am about to say will be disputed by a good many people, but I give my opinion. Many of them drink whisky when they can get it. As a race, they are fond of strong drink, but I believe that, as to sobriety, they will compare favorably with the poorer class of common laborers of any color or country. Their moral code is, it must be admitted, flexible enough to allow more margin than consists with sound ethics. Many of them have some loose notions on several of the fundamentals of morality; but they are not so bad as many have represented them to be. Many writers on the morals of the negro in the South do not consider—perhaps do not know—what are the facts in other countries as to the poorest and most ignorant of common laborers. Too much attention has been concentrated on the South for just judgments as to either the white people or the negroes. It has been like reading small type in a bright sunlight—bad reading and blurred vision.

During the past summer I passed over perhaps as many as a thousand miles of country roads by private conveyance. Some negro families I saw crowded in most wretched cabins, but they were not worse than the illustrations given in "Harper's Magazine" some months ago of attic and cellar life in New York city. Nor were they worse than the illustrations and letter-press declared to be the condition of a great multitude of families who keep miniature truck-gardens about the suburbs of our metropolis.

One of the saddest facts of their lot is that most of them are very ignorant. The vast majority of them are untaught. (Many of our white people are in the same condition.) Few ex-slaves can read at all. While slavery lasted there was small chance to teach them. For this state of things the masters were not alone to blame. Some were taught, nevertheless. It would surprise some people to know how many of them were taught by "young masters" and "young mistresses" to read the Bible. I made a faithful effort on "Uncle Jim," who taught me to ride and to plow; who was my skillful instructor in the lore of the fields and the woods. Whether he was too old, or his teacher too unskilled, has never been determined, but he never got beyond "words of one syllable." The house girl, Alice, made better progress; a sister had her schooling in hand.

A few ex-slaves have learned to read since they became free, greatly to their credit. There are some pathetic instances of old people learning, slowly and with difficulty, that they might read the Bible for themselves. Thousands of the younger race can read and write and cipher—if not after the best models, yet profitably. Some of them have learned all these things after the best models. I have examined, with a grateful heart, specimens of the work done by negro boys and girls in some of the public schools of the city of Atlanta. They were every whit as good as the best done in the white schools of similar grade. And thousands more of them will learn. Some of them "hunger and thirst" after knowledge. One of the most encouraging indications of their progress and uplifting is this: it is fast becoming a "point of honor" with colored parents that their children learn to read and to write. This sentiment is entering into their "society." Of this there can be no doubt.

Alas, that there ever was any hinderance to their education! God be thanked! there is now, January, 1881, next to no opposition to their instruction. Where one benighted neighborhood can be found where their education is opposed, twenty may be found where it is encouraged.

In closing this chapter, that is designed to give only a general statement and rough outline-sketch of their present condition and characteristics, a few words should be added as to their dispositions and tempers. They are kind-hearted, generous to the distressed, obliging, unrevengeful. They love their friends and forgive their enemies more promptly and truly than do many who have had better culture. Their disposition to help one another is a wonder. In this little village of Oxford I have seen, time and again, very poor negroes helping some of their neighbors still poorer than themselves. They have organized many "societies" for the relief of the sick and the afflicted. Many times I have known "burial expenses" met by these societies. And there can be little doubt that their "finances" are generally well and faithfully managed. One of their "treasurers" has been for some years a trusted member of my household. He has given me insight of their methods. If he were not an honest man, as he is, he has to give such rigid account that he would have little opportunity for "financiering" on the society's funds, even if he had the disposition. The picture must not be drawn in colors too bright, for, alas! a colored treasurer now and then imitates some white treasurer or cashier so closely that the society's funds are seen no more by the society forever. This, however, should be said for the negroes in such a case: they call their unfaithful treasurer "a thief," they do not say "defaulter."

3

HERE TO STAY

So far as man can see or devise, these negroes are in "the South" to stay. Common sense, in considering this problem, cannot assume a supernatural intervention to move them elsewhere. Left to the natural conditions that enter into such questions, there is no reason to expect that these Americanized Africans will remove or be removed from the regions where we now find the great mass of them. If such a not-to-be-expected migration should occur, still leaving them within the United States, the problems that grow out of their presence in this country must be worked out all the same. Change of place can no more eliminate this factor in our national equation than it can change the past history of these people in the United States.

There is much reason to believe that the problem can be better solved without a change of locality. The South is best place for these emancipated negroes, and the people of the South will yet prove themselves to be, of all people in the world, the fittest to deal with this very difficult and delicate race-problem. What we want is not a change of blackboards, but a thorough study and a clear understanding of the problem itself; also, the right spirit all round.

The conditions of this problem will not be greatly modified by the so-called "exodus"—a very large word, by the way, for the fact it represents. I hold myself bound to modify my opinions in the light of new facts, for facts must govern opinions as well as silence prejudices; but as the case now is, it is very clear to me that the negroes as a body will never move to Kansas, to Indiana, to New Mexico, or to any State or Territory, either so cold in its climate, or so different in its population, or so diverse in its conditions of living, from any thing they have ever known. A few thousands may go to these States, a few thousands may scatter themselves through various northern and western States. It is desirable that they should do so; it will extend the knowledge of the difficulties of our national problem, and nurture patience in regions where patience is as much needed as "toleration" is needed in the South.

This we may certainly depend on; if the negroes were moved *en masse* to some other section of our country, they would carry their race-problem with them. The problem would, indeed be modified; perhaps it would lose none of its present difficulties; certainly it would take on some new ones. Wherever the negroes are in large numbers, there, we may be sure, are their characteristics. If they live in the midst of another race, there, also, are the characteristics of that race; and these diverse race-characteristics—for they are not the accidents of place or special conditions—must somehow adjust themselves both to their resemblances and their differences. And there are differences as well as resemblances—a simple but important fact not always considered. The differences as well as the resemblances go deeper than the skin. Whether the negroes are superior or inferior, whether better or worse than white people, it will nevertheless be admitted by candid persons that a company of negroes—if the reader please, a very small company, so small as to be socially and politically powerless—are not, in any State, or city, or town, or country hamlet in the United States, realized in the inmost consciousness of men to be just the same as white people. The negroes themselves certainly understand and recognize these differences. These differences are realized on the plantations, in the humblest relations of obscure country life, as distinctly as in Washington city, where the wisest and best people feel (January, 1881) that they will not know just how to conduct themselves if the incoming administration should appoint a worthy and capable colored Senator from Mississippi to a cabinet portfolio. How true and wise is the remark attributed to the President elect: "It is a difficult thing always to behave one's self properly."

The preposterous scheme of colonizing the whole six millions of our negro fellow-citizens in some part of the United States, as Arizona, for example, has been mentioned a few times. Such a scheme could never originate in the serious thinking of any representative Southern man. For the Southern people, with all that has been said and thought about them, know the negro too thoroughly and love him too well to wish him such a fate. What utter nonsense! what inhuman folly! A negro State! A little Africa in America! They would perish by starvation, by internal feuds, by aggression from sharpers, speculators, and "filibusters," like those who are now threatening the peace of the Indian Territory. If the lands given them were worth having, they would be taken from them; if not, they would starve. Those who know the history of our Indian problem, who know how we have failed either to govern or protect a few thousand Indians, who were never slaves, do not desire the government to undertake the management or guardianship of several millions of emancipated Africans.

A few dreamy and sentimental visionaries talk about solving the problem at one momentous stroke. "Move the whole of them to Africa; America is for white people," they tell us. While engaged on this chapter the papers brought us word that some member of Congress has actually offered some sort of a paper proposing to buy a large territory in some of the States of Central America for the wholesale colonization of the negroes! Such legislators only serve to illustrate some of the passing humors of American voters.

If it be supposed that the negroes could be persuaded to make a real "exodus," and go to Africa, or to any of these places prepared for them, it is simply a mistake. If even one man in the United States talks of their enforced colonization, he should remember that free negroes, at least, have many "rights that white men are bound to respect." The right to live where it pleases them, so long as they obey the laws, is one of these rights.

The wholesale colonization of these people in Africa is a scheme so visionary and impracticable that it does not deserve serious discussion. But it may be looked at for a moment, if only to show what some people forget when they are caught in the current of a favorite theory. Suppose we could move the whole six millions of them to Africa. What would we do with them after getting them there? Africa is a big country, and it does not belong to us. Would it do to land them wherever our ships can approach the shore, and then turn them loose, as Mr. Seth Green turns young shad loose in the rivers, to find their way to life and fortune as best they may? This would be to turn them loose to die, or to relapse into the savagery of their ancestors. But if we owned enough of Africa, desirable and healthful parts of the continent, to furnish each family a farm; if, after getting them well settled, we could secure them decent government; if we could make sure that they would not (except those who died promptly) relapse into the heathenism from which their ancestors were taken generations ago by the cruel English and New-English sailors; if, in a word, all the conditions of successful colonization could be met, how are we to get them there? Suppose we take five hundred to the ship-load, employ one hundred ships, and make two voyages each year; we could, at this rate, get across one hundred thousand annually. But they are born faster than this. If, however, all the difficulties of transportation could be overcome, the cruelty of such a wholesale deportation would be equaled by but one thing in their eventful history, namely, the cruelty of bringing them from Africa as they were brought by the slavers.

This, I think, may be settled down upon; these negroes, ever increasing, will, for the most part, stay right where they are, in the South. But if they should be, as is most unlikely, diffused with something like equality of distribution, throughout the United States, the problem would be diffused, that is all, and with much increment of confusion and difficulty.

It seems very clear; this race-problem is likely to be our problem as a Nation always. It is certainly, at this time, a problem that the whole people should, and that the Southern people must, seriously but calmly consider.

Note—After this book was written, a friend, Mr. F. R. Richardson, the Washington city correspondent of the "Atlanta Constitution," furnished me some important statistics, taken from the official records in the office of the superintendent of the last census. I quote the following statements: "The total negro population is 6,577,497. The increase in the total population during the last ten years is 30.06 per cent.; the increase in the white population is 28.82 per cent; the increase in the colored population is 34.78 per cent."

Wise people will study these figures.

4

PROVIDENCE IN THEIR LOCATION

The African slave-trade was "the sum of all villainies." One cargo of the wretched creatures I saw long years ago. It was sickening as it was devilish. Well did David Livingstone say of the slave-trade that still exists in some parts of Africa: "It is the open sore of the world." But I have not now to discuss the sins of the bad men who brought to this country several thousands of savage Africans, the progenitors of the several millions of Americanized Africans who have been so long the bone of contention in this Republic. Nor have I, at this time, to discuss the sins of the bad masters who abused their slaves, nor the virtues of the good men and women who did the best they could with an awkward and burdensome institution, handed down to them from their fathers, and fastened upon them by historical, industrial, political, and social conditions that they could not control.

In this discussion I am concerned about those facts connected with their history and present condition which may aid me in the consideration of the problem that grows out of their presence here.

They are in the United States, six and a half millions strong. Their dwelling-places are chiefly between parallels of latitude 30° and 40°, and of longitude (west of Washington) 0° and 25°, embracing, as some patriotic and perhaps enthusiastic people think, the very best part of the globe, as Goshen was the best part of Egypt.

At the first there were slaves in the Northern States, even in New England. Slavery was abolished in Massachusetts by the

State Constitution of 1780. It was not finally extinct in Connecticut until after the year 1840. "The United States Census," says Curtis, in his "History of the Constitution," vol. ii, p. 289, footnote, "for 1790 returned 2,759 slaves for Connecticut; the census for 1840 returned 17; in the census for 1850 none were returned. A like gradual emancipation took place in New Hampshire, Rhode Island, Vermont, New York and Pennsylvania." The emancipation of the slaves in these States did not produce any financial, social, or political convulsions. And chiefly for two reasons: I. There were few to set free, too few to make it profitable to keep them in servitude or perilous to emancipate and enfranchise them. 2. Their emancipation was so gradual that both masters and slaves were prepared for it. Is it surprising that the sudden emancipation of between four and five millions of slaves, at the close of an exhausting war, convulsed and prostrated the Southern States in 1865?

Slavery was unprofitable in the Northern States, and, in the course of time, the opinions and sentiments of the best people were arrayed against the institution. These opinions grew into amazing strength soon after the final abolition of slavery in the last of the Northern States. Some of their slaves lived after their emancipation in the States where they had been set free; others were sent South before their emancipation, and sold to those who still believed in the institution. In this way, in some cases at least, the ignorance and errors of one party helped another party to ease of conscience without loss of cash. I have long believed that it was one of the most fortunate things in the world that slavery did not prosper in the Northern States. If it had been profitable in the North, these good people, according to the infirmity of our nature, might possibly have remained to this day unconvinced of the evils of slavery, being blinded by their worldly interests. Had slavery been profitable in the North, the institution, with all its evils, might have been fixed upon this country, so far as human purposes might have had to do with the matter, forever.

Most sincerely do I believe that this would have been not only a grievous misfortune, but a withering curse. If slavery had damaged the whole of the Union as it undoubtedly damaged the South, what a loss to the world! Well may we admire the resources of the divine Providence that works vast moral revolutions out of the failure of men's devices. After slavery failed in the North it was doomed in the South.

It has been a dark and troubled question to thousands of as honest and godly people as ever sought the truth, fought for what they believed to be the right, or worshiped God; yet who can tell but that the failure of the Southern Confederacy may yet, in the wise and gracious Providence that overrules the nations, bring as great blessings to the South as the failure of slavery brought blessings to the North? If it shall turn out so, our children's children will celebrate the surrender at Appomattox as a day of blessing, although they will still honor the spirit of the men who won the praise of the world for their heroic struggles for what was dear to their love and their faith.

If it shall be asked, How came these poor Africans to this country? I answer, without hesitation, *God brought them here, "to save much people alive."* I do not say that the merciful and just God sanctioned the slave-trade. For that was one of the darkest crimes recorded on the page of history. But there is no doctrine more clearly taught in the Holy Scriptures than that God "makes the wrath of man to praise him:" that he overrules the selfishness and sins of men to bring about good and gracious results. On this rock has triumphant faith ten thousand times planted her feet in the day of darkness and doubt.

Let us illustrate the doctrine:

Joseph was carried into Egypt as a slave, and sold by his blood-brothers to wandering merchants of the Arabs. What a light is cast upon dark providences by the words of good and wise Joseph to his penitent brethren when they had returned to Egypt from the burial of their father Jacob: "As for you, ye thought evil against me; but God meant it unto good, to bring to pass, as it is this day, to save much people alive." And what blessings, reaching wide, did this Joseph, stolen from his father, sold into slavery by his brothers, bring not only to his father's house, but to Egypt, the land of his servitude!

All providences, in the lives of individuals and in the history of nations, must be interpreted in the light of their relation to the Cross of Christ, which shines backward and forward upon all the dark questions of the ages. Let us try to look at the question, first, of African slavery, and, secondly, of African freedom in the United States, in this clear and steady light.

The secular historian will say truly that the negroes did a wonderful work in helping to subdue this western wilderness. But the historian of the Church of Christ and the recorder of the great deeds in true human progress, will say that the most wonderful of all facts connected with the strange history of the children of Africa in America is this: that there are now, 1881, nearly one million of them in the communion of the various Christian Churches in the United States, and that the six millions of them have been brought largely under the influence of the Christian religion. Immortal is the honor that belongs to the memory of the Christian men and women of the South who, long before 1865, so preached the Gospel to the slaves upon the plantations, that nearly half a million of them were brought into the different Churches that were then at work in the Southern States. And immortal is the honor due to those who, taking up the good work where the men and women of the South were, by the circumstances of an evil time, compelled to lay it down for awhile, (it is only for awhile,) have carried it on so well that in fifteen years they have added nearly half a million more to the number of believing negroes.

Weak and foolish are they who sneer at the religion of negroes. It is true that they may have vague ideas of "dogma"; they may not use a dignified "liturgy" in their worship; they may have more emotion than "esthetics" in their religion; but this fact remains—they are not heathens. They are as far above and beyond their heathen forefathers as the most cultured of English-speaking people are superior to the Britons, long after Cæsar's invasion.

Seeing that the greatest fact of the history of African slavery in the United States is the Christianizing of hundreds of thousands of them, I conclude that Christianizing them was the grand providential design in their coming to this country. It is, by the way, a significant fact, that the wild Africans appeared on these shores long before there was a thought of a Foreign Missionary Society in the American Churches. Who knows but that the heathen who were brought to us largely moved the Churches to send the Gospel to the heathen in their own lands? He who cannot, through all the mists and clouds of this strange and troubled history, see the hand of God in their coming to this country, can hardly understand the "going down" of Israel "into Egypt."

Let us refer to that history a moment. God would "raise up a peculiar people." The problem of a Hebrew race, of comparatively pure blood, could not have been worked out in Canaan, with its roving shepherd life. As far back as the "call" of Abraham out of "Ur of the Chaldees" we see the hand of Providence in manifold adjustments that issued in separating this one family from their fire-worshiping kindred the other side of the Euphrates. The same design is manifested in God's dealing with the larger family of Jacob. To preserve them a "peculiar people" they were, under pressure of famine, moved into Egypt, where, in many providential ways, they were cared for—"nourished" is Joseph's word—and protected till the family grew into a tribe, the tribe into a race, a nation within a nation, but yet not strong enough, in numbers or character, to be transplanted to the promised land. The problem needed Egypt, fertile and favorable to the rapid increase of the race, and, as the strongest of the nations, able to protect the children of Israel from their enemies. It needed, also, a people who, by tradition, hated "shepherds," and who, when they came to fear their increasing strength, made them slaves. The Hebrew slavery and the Egyptian caste-prejudice against foreigners and shepherds conspired to keep the races unmixed. If there had been free intermarriage the Hebrew race would have been absorbed within the first hundred years of their stay in Egypt, and the whole problem lost irretrievably.

A good deal has been said at random, and in a declamatory way, about the iniquity of caste. May be we have not yet reached the bottom of this subject; may be, if God had designed any such commingling of bloods as would issue in one conglomerate race, there never would have been any such sentiment or instinct in the human breast.

Let us suppose now that one hundred thousand Africans—heathen all—had been set down in America about the time the children of the Pilgrim Fathers were getting a foothold in Massachusetts and the Cavaliers were establishing their settlements in Virginia and the Carolinas; and suppose there had not been, as there was from the beginning, spontaneous and resistless, one instinct of caste attraction and repulsion, and that there had been no obstacle to free intermarriage. Very soon there would have been no African race in this country. The issue would have been largely different; there would have been no heathen African race to train to useful arts, sturdy strength, and manly character, to lift up and to Christianize; but a Christian white race might have been largely heathenized. How would such a mingling of bloods as is here supposed have effected the development of civilization in the United States? It is a question that one who loves free institutions and has hope that his country holds a blessing for the world, does not like to consider.

Furthermore, had such an issue followed the introduction of the heathen negroes into this country, there would have been for continental Africa, with her uncounted millions, no morning star of hope shining over the lowly cabins and humble sanctuaries of their Christianized brethren in America. For we must never forget the ultimate outcome of this vast movement; we must never forget that the Christianizing of these multitudes of Africans here looks, and must look, to the salvation of the vaster multitudes in Africa itself. And in order to work out these results, both here and yonder, it was necessary to preserve a comparatively pure African race in this country. In those cases where human sin has mixed these diverse bloods the divine plan, I must believe, has been so much marred. But, as to the great majority of them, the Africans in this country are, as we have seen, pure bloods. The caste feeling and the environments of slavery favored this design of Providence in a far greater degree than those persons suppose who do not thoroughly know the negro in the rural districts of the South, as well as in the towns and cities.

But why should the South be the chosen field for working out this stupendous race-problem that involves, as surely as the world moves or stands, the destiny of two continents? All the reasons I claim not to have discovered; some, doubtless, are as yet undeveloped; but some of them seem very plain to me.

1. These African children, in the school of Providence, needed a warm climate. The South gave them a better climate than Africa could give. And one result among many is, the descendants of the wild Africans that first landed on these shores are, in every respect, a finer race than were their ancestors when they came, than are their kindred who still inhabit the original dwelling-places of their people. In horticultural gardens tender exotic plants are sometimes hardened by frequent transplantings. So these Africans, who were brought to America, found a climate that was warm enough to suit their constitution, and that was yet free from the enervating heats of the tropics. The wisdom of Providence is justified in an improved and bettered race.

2. They needed, for a time, the guidance and protection of a stronger people. And, they needed, in order that the best results might follow, in this stronger race, a people of homogeneous blood. They found such a race in the Southern whites as they could have found it nowhere else in the United States. Thus, in Georgia, according to the Census of 1880, there is a total population of 1,538,983. Of the whole number only 10,310 are foreigners. In further illustration it may be mentioned that in Louisiana, where there was not a homogeneous white race, the Christianizing process did not succeed nearly so well as in South Carolina, where nearly all the white people were English, or in Georgia, where, as we have seen, the foreign element in the population is, practically an inappreciable quantity. How our difficult problem would be complicated were there in the States where the freed negroes are a dense foreign population! Only suppose an Irish ward in New York or Philadelphia, or a German ward in Chicago or Cincin-

nati, outworked, under-bid, and out-voted by a "solid" black column! There would be blood and chaos.

3. They needed in the religion of the ruling race a Protestant faith, pure and simple. They found such a Protestantism in the South as they could have found it nowhere else in the world. It may be one of the blessings of Southern provincialism that the many speculative vagaries that have plagued the Church in Germany, in England, and in New England, have never prospered in the Southern States of the Union. No form of infidelity has ever had welcome, or won a foothold, among the people of the South. And, with the exception of the French-settled State of Louisiana, Romanism has never had dominion in these States. I do not wish to say what may offend pious Roman Catholics, but I refer to matters of history when I say that, as compared with the influence of Protestantism upon Africans held in slavery, Romanism has notably failed. Witness Louisiana in the United States; the West India Islands, except in those members of this group where the English flag gave liberty and opportunity to Protestant missionaries. Witness, also, Mexico, the Central American States, and the Empire of Brazil.

4. They needed protection against the worst instincts of the stronger race itself; this they received through the self-interest—for slavery was profitable in the South—if not through the humanity, of their masters. That there were many exceptions to this rule I allow and deplore. But perhaps one would not go too far were he to say, If it was needful for these men in stature and children in intelligence to have masters, for a time, the Southern whites made as good masters as they could have found in any country.

Alas! many of these masters did not recognize the divine hand in the wonderful providences of this strange history; many of them did not realize their sacred function of "school-masters" to bring these children of the sun to Christ. *But many of them did, and they were faithful to God and to their servants.* Wherein any of them sinned against God in sinning against their dark-skinned brother, alas! they were not alone. Southern masters were not alone in dealing hardly with dependents. "Let him that is without sin"—let him only—"cast the first stone." May I not add this word also?—wherein any have sinned all have suffered. For every wrong done to defenseless slaves the whole race of masters paid a penalty, of which the loss of money was unspeakably the lesser part. For every mercy shown the slave, for every kind word, for every effort to lift him up, for every brotherly office, the good and just God gives the master full recognition and approbation. Men have not always treated the master so justly; they could not, for they saw only in part; and the better part, from their distant point of view and their uncertain lights, they could not see. I know that in very many Southern homes (scores I could name in these pages—my honored and translated father's among them) in the old days, the servants made part of the worshiping household, and that behind them, as they sung or knelt at the family altar, the devout master saw "Ethiopia stretching out her hands."

The outcome of it all is, the one million communicants and the six millions more or less "leavened" by Christian principle and sentiment. If there is such a fact in Christian history I know not where it is recorded.

The religion of the Southern negroes—slave or free—was, and is, a divine reality. During the late war their religion was pure and strong enough to secure to helpless women and children, on the Southern plantations, peace and safety, while the men were in the Southern armies fighting under a flag which did not promise freedom to the slaves. And we may be quite sure that the negroes understood what the war meant in its relation to them. In what history can the conduct of these Southern slaves, from 1861 to 1865, be matched? There are three explanations: 1. The negro is not naturally daring or revengeful. 2. The majority of them loved their owners. 3. Multitudes of them were truly religious.

In trying to understand the coming of these African slaves to America and their settlement and history in the South, we must remember these one million of communicants; this whole race more or less influenced by the gospel leaven; we must also consider what these American-African Christians may some day do for Africa.

5

THE NEGRO FREE

One may be entirely consistent when he says, I recognize the hand of Providence in the coming to this country of several thousands of savage and heathen Africans; I recognize the hand of Providence in the circumstances of their enslavement, in such a country and among such a people, and I rejoice now, and thank God, from day to day, that this same Providence has set them free forever. If any object, he must say, "Either Providence was not in their coming, their enslavement, or their emancipation." He who says either of these things has given up the Bible and the rational doctrine of Providence. For one, I do not believe that the Providence that includes "lilies" and "sparrows" overlooks millions of human beings.

As to slavery itself, I do not discuss it. The sins connected with it every good man deplores; for the blessings God brought the negroes while in slavery—whether by virtue of it, or in spite of it—every good man, who has knowledge of the facts, gives thanks to the Giver of all good. I am not called on to discuss the right or wrong of slavery. I will not discuss dead issues while there are more living ones than we can manage. In this discussion my chief concern is not with slavery, but with the facts that grow out of its abolition. I have nothing to do with slavery, except only as its facts and issues affect us of to-day. I say "us." I mean the negroes and the white people of this whole Nation. I am not, in the least degree, responsible for the introduction of African slaves into this country; I am not responsible for being born in a slave-holding community; I am not responsible for being born the son of a slave-holder—a man who feared God and "served his generation according to the will of God," who never treated a slave unjustly or unkindly, and who was followed to his grave (December 26, 1862) with their loud lamentations. Let it be remembered that of the white people of the South who are now suffering so many of the ills of slavery, who are now paying, in a hundred ways, so fearful a price for the imposition of slavery upon the very civil and social institutions under which they were born—let it be remembered that the majority of these people *never did own slaves.* Let it be remembered, also, that of those who must now bear the responsibilities of citizenship, who must now, through a thousand struggles, and against a thousand adverse minds, win for their section of the Union what, but for slavery, they would have inherited—let it be remembered that the majority of these men have "come of age" since 1861. And let those men who, so far as their civil life is concerned, were "born free" from the entanglements of slavery, remember, also, that they are not of the past, but of the present and the future; let them remember that God has set *them* free as well as the negroes, and that now the "truth" should "make them free" altogether and forever.

Again I say, I will not discuss the dead and buried slavery. If slavery must be discussed, there are plenty of people who are masters of the argument; plenty of people who have delight in it. One may, it is to be hoped, in such a country and in such an age as this rejoice that the negroes are "free," without being required, in order to prove his sincerity, to condemn the memory of his fathers, who conscientiously believed that they ought not to be set free. I will neither malign nor condemn the memory of my fathers, for I cannot forget that the Federal Constitution, which not only recognized slavery, but inwrought it into the very bone and fiber and blood of our institutions, was framed nearly one hundred years ago. But I do rejoice in the emancipation of the negroes. To ask a Southern man to denounce the past history of his people, because he recognizes the facts of the present and believes in the possibilities of the coming time, would be as reasonable as to require a son of the Pilgrim Fathers to vindicate his present intolerance of persecution by declaring Cotton Mather to have been a hypocrite and a villain.

There is no more slavery in our country. The former advocates of slavery—such of them as are still alive, for the majority of them are *dead*—fully accept emancipation. Let the former advocates of emancipation accept it also, and have done with digging up slavery as an everlasting theme of anniversary orations. It would be just as sensible to denounce George III. on every anniversary of American Independence. Now his Majesty George III. is dead and buried; let him rest. We would suspect one of poverty of intellectual resources if he found himself unable to get through a "Fourth-of-July" speech without making faces and hurling epithets at the poor old king. It is said that the monarchists, when Charles II was restored to his father's throne, dug up the bones of Cromwell and hung them on Tyburn Hill. It was not statesmanship but passion that did this. True wisdom, to say nothing of magnanimity, would have left his bones in their grave. Even slavery is entitled to its grave. In that grave, for it is very deep, both parties should bury their quarrel, without resurrection.

Slavery is done with. The negroes have been set free once and for all, as every body knows. It is done, and it will never be undone. There are many reasons for this opinion. Three I mention: First, If there were any to desire their re-enslavement, they know full well that the might and conscience of the Christian world are against it. There is no fool mad enough to breast a tidal wave that moves with the force of a whole ocean. Secondly, Their re-enslavement is not desired. The few "old masters" who still live—and let it be remembered by just men that most of them are dead—do not desire it. (I have known but one man among the "old masters" who said he wished his slaves again. He said this a few months after Appomattox. In less than twelve months he was elected to office by negro votes!) Thirdly, Every body knows, fully and definitely, that the re-enslavement of these freed negroes cannot, by any possibility, be brought about. One of the wants of our generation is silence on this subject. It is not only true that the Southern people do not desire the re-enslavement of the negroes, but it is true, also, as has been mentioned, that the majority of Southern people never owned slaves, and it is further true, that thousands upon thousands of them never believed in the institution, and they ask on this subject silence. Are they not entitled to ask this much?

I do not claim to have been among those who never believed in slavery. Time was when I did believe in it thoroughly, and when I defended it to the best of my ability. I make no apology for having believed in it. I was taught to believe in it; I grew up in the midst of it; I saw its very best aspects in my father's house. His slaves loved me, and I loved them; and we love each other to-day. Nor do I make any apology for saying, I do not now believe in slavery. I have changed my opinions; rather, new and purer light has changed them. "Truly the light is sweet, and a pleasant thing it is for the eyes to behold the sun."

But I will not denounce the "old masters"; I will not discuss slavery. It is infinitely more important to this generation, infinitely more important for the generations that come after us, that we discuss the negro's freedom. On this subject we want light, clear and steady. We cannot study this lesson by the light of camp fires; we need the pure white light of the sun. And it is a more difficult subject than slavery; it is in a hundred ways involved and complicated. It is a subject that cannot be mastered in the heats of sectional or party passion. It requires the poise of good sense and the guidance of good conscience following, through a tangled wilderness, the pure light of a fixed star. It is time now that men should study this question, in all its relations, calmly and justly. Nearly half the life of a generation has been lived since the echoes of the last battle of the horrible civil war died away. We are moving out of the century which quarreled and fought and offered up the lives of thousands of its best and bravest in the final settlement of the dispute. The gray light of the dawning of the twentieth century appears in the eastern sky; there is the song of morning birds in the air; presently the rosy day will burst upon us. In God's name let us every one—men of the North and men of the South—get ready for the coming day.

To the subject of African freedom, then, in all its relations to two races, to two continents, and to the world, I am willing to give my best attention, see king the fullest truth in the purest light God may give me. And I know, by the authority of Christ, my Lord, that the "truth makes free." I know, also, that nothing else makes free in this world. Arguments, laws, proclamations, amendments to constitutions, battles; these alone make no man free. The truth, and nothing else, makes free the souls as well as the bodies of men.

There are three parties in this great historic conflict that need freedom by the truth: the men of the South, the men of the North, and the negroes themselves. Let no man flatter himself that he knows all the truth of this deep and difficult problem. I know that I do not. "I count not myself to have apprehended: but this one thing I do, forgetting those things which are behind, and reaching forth unto those things which are before, I press toward the mark for the prize of my high calling of God in Christ Jesus."

6

PROVIDENCE IN EMANCIPATION

In this discussion I have to do with African slavery only in so far as slavery was used by the mysterious but all-wise and gracious providence of God to prepare the negroes for their freedom. Nay, more than this, for what is of vaster import, to prepare them for their duties and destiny in the right use of their freedom. Is this a fancy? Is this a mere vagary of Southern prejudice? When I say that God used their slavery to prepare them for their freedom, am I only seeking a sort of last refuge for an opinion on the subject of slavery that I have affirmed that I have utterly given up and changed? Nay, verily, I recognize the obvious facts of the history of the negro race in America. Nor are these facts exceptional. God never gave freedom to any barbarous nation without first subjecting them, in some way, to a period and a discipline of preparation. No savage people ever sprang at a bound into the enjoyment of freedom, and held it long, or used it wisely. Most republics have failed because the people were not ready for them. Heaven judged that a period of four hundred years was not too long to prepare the Hebrew race for independent national life. The records of Exodus show that even they had not learned too well the providential lessons of their stay in "the house of bondage."

Let me ask, and let sober people answer, whether the wild Africans were fitted for freedom when they were first landed from the slave-ships that brought them from their savage homes to the plantations of this country. Were not their American masters, unworthy of their sacred trust as many of them were, better fitted, judged by any test, to prepare these people for freedom than were their African masters and conquerors who sold them to the slavers? For what is generally forgotten should be always remembered—most of the negroes sold into slavery in America were bought from slavery in Africa. And surely I do not go too far when I say, American slavery was freedom compared with the slavery from which they were taken.

Some of them, I know, were not technically slaves in their own country; some were bought as captives taken in predatory wars; some of them were stolen from their homes. If slavery in Africa were considered by those who say so much of the evils of American slavery, they would at least find reasons to magnify the Providence that so overruled the cupidity and cruelty of wicked men as to bring the divinest blessings, for both worlds, to the helpless victims of their sin.

The poor Africans were not, as every candid man will admit, as well fitted for freedom when the slave-ships first landed them in America as they were when God gave them their freedom in 1865. Only suppose they had been set free when first they came. Does any rational man suppose there would have been so good an outcome? We are not lacking in a historic parallel. The red men were here when the "Mayflower" came, and when the Cavaliers first founded their colonies. And they were always free. They have never been subjected to personal slavery. The Indians were never less civilized than were the Africans at their coming to our country. But what blessings has their freedom brought them? Were they not slain, tribe after tribe? Have they increased in numbers? Have they been Christianized? Has not this "Indian question" been, from the beginning, the shame and perplexity and despair of our statesmanship? Have we mastered this question after two hundred years of blundering experiment? Let any man imagine, who can and who dares, what would have been the fate of a few thousand Africans, ignorant, debased, and *idolatrous,* turned loose to freedom when their feet first touched our shores.

There can be no doubt that in the minds of nearly all of the negroes of this country that very remarkable and historic man, Abraham Lincoln, is loved and revered as their deliverer. They accept and honor him as the "Moses" of their salvation. Never can I forget the countenance of a negro man I saw one day in March, 1875, contemplating a statue of Mr. Lincoln in the Rotunda of the Capitol in Washington city. Evidently he was not a resident in the city. Like myself, he was a visitor, seeing what he could. It may be counted a weakness or a want of taste in me, but no matter; of all things I saw in Washington city, that negro's countenance most impressed me, and it is now my most vivid remembrance. He stood still and silent before the voiceless marble, gazing at it as if he would read the very soul of the man it represented. His face and attitude moved me deeply. It was plain that the negro wanted to talk to the statue; that he longed to bless with loving thanks the man who made him free. I was not mistaken in his feeling. I know the negro face. There was something almost worshipful in the man's manner and expression as he stood in silent contemplation. He looked as if the sight of that marble statue was the fruition of a pilgrimage, and as if he felt that he stood on "holy ground." That man represented the feeling of his race. All over the South the name of Abraham Lincoln is, to the negroes, the name of a saint and martyr of God. They are in singular ignorance of the men and women who nobly fought their battles. Garrison, Sumner, Seward, and Greeley are names that, to the mass of them, are unknown. But the name of Abraham Lincoln is engraved on all their hearts. It is not surprising that they should know him only, or that they should almost worship his memory.

Many of the negroes look beyond Mr. Lincoln for the gift of their freedom; they look upon him as the instrument of the divine Providence. But the majority of them do not look beyond the instrument. It seems to me a matter of vast moment to both races that the hand of God should be recognized in this whole history—one of the most remarkable that belongs to the annals of any nation. It is important to the emancipated negro to see God in his freedom, that there may be in his heart and life a right conscience in the use of his freedom. This lesson a few of them—very few, I fear—have learned. The majority accept the fact, in a blind sort of way, as deliverance from restraint, as license to do what they will. But their freedom can never bring them its fullness of blessing till the heart of the emancipated race is penetrated and saturated with this conception: "The good hand of God is in all our history; he overruled the slavers who brought us here; he overruled slavery; he gave us our freedom."

I would not diminish their gratitude to Mr. Lincoln or to the party he represented; I would be glad if I could deepen their gratitude to God.

It is equally important, so far as their duties to the negroes are concerned, that the people of the North and of the South recognize God's hand in his providential dealings both with slavery and its termination.

There has been, I must believe, much sin and unbelief, as well as confusion of thought, on both sides in our attitude toward this subject of the emancipation of the slaves. In the North, with many notable exceptions, there has been much boasting and self-laudation. Where men ought to feel humbly that God has used them—used them in their weakness and folly, as well as in their strength and wisdom—as unworthy instruments to accomplish a great design, they have boasted overmuch in their triumph over their late antagonists in a fierce and bloody war. Sometimes, alas! there has flamed out in sermons and orations and essays somewhat of the fatal pride of Nebuchadnezzar, intoxicated with his greatness: "Is not this great Babylon, that I have built for the house of the kingdom by the might of my power, and for the honor of my majesty?" Proud and weak man, he had forgotten his vision of the great tree and of the warning cry of "the watchers and the holy one."

The men of the North can never realize the vast import of the freedom of the negroes in America so long as they indulge a spirit so boastful and proud of their own relations to emancipation. Nor can they realize their high duties to this race, whose preparation for a great future has been only begun.

We of the South have not been without folly and unbelief and sin in or attitude toward this fact of emancipation. We have been slow to accept its full significance even when we fully and finally accepted the fact. It was not unnatural that we felt bitterly the humiliations of our overthrow, nor that we writhed in agony when we looked upon the poverty and desolation of our land when it was all over. It was not unnatural that our people were slow to accept the issues of the war. (I am not speaking of what was wise, but of what is natural.) It was not unnatural that we felt ourselves goaded to desperation by many of the requirements and events of reconstruction. History will not deny that there were unnecessary exasperations in many of the methods employed to settle the questions that grew out of the war. Rarely have a brave and high-spirited people endured such trials of their patience, their wisdom, and their faith. For many follies we committed, for many wrongs that were done by some people of the South, there is no defense to be made. Nor can defense be made for many of the acts of the conquerors that drove Southern men to desperation. Earth and Heaven know there were wrongs and sins enough on both sides to leave small room for boasting to either.

When all the facts are considered, those who know human nature will feel no surprise that the South has been slow and reluctant to adjust itself to the new order of things. As it seems to me one of the many sad effects of our unhappy experience has been that the light has been dimmed in which we ought to have seen the hand of God, and read the lessons of his providence. As a wise and saintly man, whose calm soul has been lifted above the passions of the hour, recently wrote to me: "Our new position has been forced upon us, and in several respects tyrannically forced, so that we have come slowly to see Providence in the change. With bayonets between Providence and ourselves it was very hard to see the good in and through the evil. Large allowance should be made for this." I believe God does make allowance, and so ought men.

Nevertheless, it is our sacred duty to see God wherever God is. How can the people of the South ever understand this "negro question"—both slavery and emancipation—until they recognize God's hand in this long and troubled history? I do not mean recognize God's approval of all things, but God's providence in all things—masterful, comprehensive, overruling, all-wise, and good.

This much to me is clear; until God's hand in this whole history is recognized, neither the men of the North nor the men of the South will or can make the right use of the negro's freedom.

There can be no question, I think, but that emancipation was set down in the order of divine Providence. Had the white people realized, both in thought and act, their relation to the slaves, emancipation might have come sooner, it might have come later, but it would have come peaceably, and when both masters and slaves were better prepared for the change. It is to me a very painful thought that, while there were very many noble exceptions, the majority of masters never understood the solemnity of their trust in the temporary guardianship of these negroes in course of training. Many of them, I fear the larger number, recognized chiefly a property interest in the negroes. Men with this feeling uppermost could not do their duty to the slaves. But God's plans must not be marred by human ignorance or cupidity. So it came to pass that God used a great war to set free the negroes.

If the hand of God were fully and devoutly recognized by all parties—by the people of the North, by the people of the South, and by the negroes—only the happiest results would follow. When this truth shines clearly upon us all there will be peace and brotherhood. This truth will drive out passion and prejudice. The man of the North will be less boastful and imperious, less self-satisfied and Pharisaical in his attitude toward the South. No offense is intended by the use of this word Pharisaical. Its application is not meant for all Northern men, for many have seen too much of the true light to indulge the spirit of self-complacency. I use the word because I know of no other that so truly expresses the spirit of many Northern men—of many, too, who hold high place and mold public opinion—in their long-indulged habit of looking upon the South as a sort of national Nazareth. I put it to their consciences whether they have not overmuch and over-often indulged the spirit and used the words of him who went not "down to his house justified:" "God, I thank thee, that I am not as other men are, ...or even as this publican?"

I would not do the North injustice, nor would I claim over-much for the South. Southern faults I do not deny; Northern excellencies I do not disparage. I know the faults of the Southern people better than men of the North know them, and I feel them more keenly, because, alas! part of them are my own.

If all of superiority they of the North claim be granted, (and they are superior to us in many things, though not in all,) and their theory of the evils of slavery be true—which I accept for the most part—then where is there occasion for boasting? Had slavery been fastened on New England for generations, are the men of New England prepared to prove, beyond all question, that they would now be so much better than they think the South is? Should they not, in gratitude for deliverance from the curse of slavery long years before the South got its release, be less impatient with those who, according to their own view of the evils of slavery, could not be much better than they are? What would we think of the wisdom, to say nothing of his spirit, of a missionary who should begin his labors in a heathen land by not only proving idolatry to be a lie, but by denouncing the low estate of the people whom that idolatry had degraded? Have they ever considered fairly that, had the relations of the sections to slavery been changed, had the South been freed from slavery in 1790, and New England burdened with it till 1865, they might have been as deficient in the virtues of the best civilization as they believe that the South is, and the South might have excelled as they believe that they have excelled? In such a case, what would the golden rule require of the South?

When we of the South recognize, as we ought, the providence of God in the emancipation of the negroes, most gracious results will follow in us. The spirit of resignation to God's will in this matter will go further than any thing conceivable by me to reconcile us to the instrument employed by that Providence. Such a spirit would go far to banish whatever "wrath and bitterness" there may be in us. It will broaden our views; it will lift us up to a higher plane of thought and sentiment and conduct.

When the negroes come to see, as I trust they may, that God set them free, only using men and their counsels as his instruments, then a new and holier feeling will come into their hearts. They cannot realize the solemn significance of their freedom so long as they forget their great Deliverer in their over consideration of the instrument he employed.

The emancipated negro can never have the right conscience in his freedom, can never realize in his inmost soul the responsibilities of his freedom, can never perform aright the duties of free citizenship, can never work out the divine plan of his destiny, until he sees clearly and feels profoundly that God, the Father and King of men, bestowed upon him this fearful but glorious gift of freedom.

7

THE EMANCIPATION PROCLAMATION

That Mr. Lincoln was truly opposed to slavery, and that he wished and sought its abolition, cannot be doubted. That he issued his Emancipation Proclamation simply or chiefly in the interests of the slaves, and in order to set them free, his own words deny. His grand aim was to "save the Union," and he issued his proclamations to help in saving it. This subject is brought forward here only because it should, when fully understood, deepen and fix the conviction that God, and not man, gave freedom to the slaves.

In the "North American Review" for February, 1880, is an interesting and instructive article on the Emancipation Proclamation from the pen of President James C. Welling, who was, at the time it was issued, one of the editors of the "Intelligencer," Washington city, and whose opportunities for full information were complete. Commenting on this article in the "North American Review" for August, 1800, Mr. Richard H. Dana commends it very highly, and says: "It presents the subject with great ability and fullness of detail, and, as far as my memory goes, it is the first article in an American periodical that has taken up the subject on principle."

Of the Proclamation itself President Welling says:

The Emancipation Proclamation is the most signal fact in the administration of President Lincoln. It marks, indeed, the sharp

and abrupt beginning of 'the Great Divide' which, since the upheaval produced by the late civil war, has separated the polity
and politics of the *ante-bellum* period from the polity and politics
of the *post-bellum* era. No other act has been so warmly praised
on the one hand, or so warmly opposed on the other; and perhaps it has sometimes been equally misunderstood, in its real
nature and bearing, by those who have praised it and by those
who have denounced it. The domestic institution against which
it was leveled having now passed as finally into the domain of
history as the slavery of Greece and Rome, it would seem that
the time has come when we can review this act of Mr. Lincoln's
in the calm light of reason, without serious disturbance from the
illusions of fancy or the distortions of prejudice.

In the latter part of August, 1862, Mr. Horace Greeley, editor of the "New York Tribune," wrote an editorial in his paper in
which, as President Welling says, "assuming to utter the prayer of
twenty millions, Mr. Greeley called on the President with much
truculence of speech, to issue a proclamation of freedom to all
slaves in the Confederate States." On the 22nd of the month Mr.
Lincoln replied to Mr. Greeley's editorial through the "Intelligencer," published in Washington city. It is a remarkable and
interesting document. It was written about one month before
the appearance of Mr. Lincoln's preliminary Proclamation, in
which he gave the Confederates notice that if they did not, in
one hundred days, lay down their arms and give up their cause,
he would proclaim freedom to all the slaves in the States at war
with the Union forces. The "North American Review" gives us an
engraved copy, a *fac-simile* of Mr. Lincoln's letter to Mr. Greeley,
just as it appeared in the "Intelligencer." It is straightforward, unmistakable; it tells exactly what the great war President thought
and felt and purposed in the Proclamations of Emancipation that
appeared soon after. It is a most readable letter, aside from its
historical interest. Comparatively few of the present generation,
especially in the Southern States of the Union, have read it. It may
not be out of place to reproduce it here. I give it in full, using Mr.
Lincoln's italics:

EXECUTIVE MANSION, WASHINGTON, August 22, 1862

HON. HORACE GREELEY:

DEAR SIR: I have just read yours of the 19th, addressed to myself through the "New York Tribune." If there be in it any statements or assumption of facts which I may know to be erroneous, I do not, now and here, controvert them. If there be in it any inferences which I may believe to be falsely drawn, I do not, now and here, argue against them. If there be perceptible in it an imperious and dictatorial tone, I waive it in deference to an old friend, whose heart I have always supposed to be right.

As to the policy I seem to be pursuing, as you say, I have not meant to leave any one in doubt.

I would save the Union. I would save it the shortest way under the Constitution. The sooner the national authority can be restored the nearer the Union will be 'the Union as it was.' [Here is a sentence marked out in the engraved copy, because the editors of the "Intelligencer" insisted that it was not dignified enough for such a paper: "Broken eggs can never be mended, and the longer the breaking proceeds the more will be broken."] If there be those who would not save the Union, unless they could at the same time *destroy* slavery, I do not agree with them. My paramount object in this struggle *is* to save the Union, and is *not* either to save or to destroy slavery. If I could save the Union without freeing *any* slave I would do it, and if I could save it by freeing *all* the slaves I would do it; and if I could save it by freeing some and leaving others alone I would also do that. What I do about slavery and the colored race, I do because I believe it helps to save the Union; and what I forbear I forbear because I do *not* believe it would help to save the Union. I shall do *less* whenever I shall believe what I am doing hurts the cause, and I shall do *more* whenever I shall believe doing more will help the cause. I shall try to correct errors when shown to be errors; and I shall adopt new views so fast as they shall appear to be true views.

I have here stated my purpose according to my view of *official* duty; and I intend no modification of my oft-expressed *personal* wish that all men, every-where, should be free.

Yours,

A. LINCOLN

This is, in many respects, a very notable letter. It is wholly characteristic of its remarkable author, whose assassination has been mourned by millions of Southern people, not only on account of the dastardly crime of his murder, but because the wiser ones among them have long ago settled down into the belief that, in the death of Abraham Lincoln, they lost one who would have dealt with them in the spirit of his own beautiful words, "*With malice toward none, with charity for all.*"

This is clear: the *man*, Abraham Lincoln, wished all slaves to be free; the *President* put the Union before all things. If freeing them would help to save the Union, he would free them; if to save the Union it had been necessary to keep all of them, or part of them, in slavery, he would keep them in slavery. And in point of historic fact the Emancipation Proclamation, when it came, did not propose to set all the slaves free; in Maryland and Kentucky, and in all the slave States not recognized officially as being in rebellion, the slaves were slaves. The Proclamation was hurled at "rebellion," not at slavery. Nothing can be plainer than this. On the 10th of March, 1862, President Welling says,

> Mr. Lincoln had said that as long as he remained President the people of Maryland (and, therefore, of the Border States) had nothing to fear for their peculiar domestic institution, "either by direct action of the government or by indirect action, or through the emancipation of slaves in the District of Columbia, or the confiscation of Southern property in slaves."

Mr. Lincoln had little faith in the Proclamation's bringing any deliverance to the slaves. On the 13th of September, 1862, nine days before the "Preliminary Proclamation" was issued, a delegation of Chicago clergymen waited upon the President, urging him strenuously to issue a proclamation freeing the slaves. He answered them:

> What good would a proclamation of emancipation from me do, especially as we are now situated? I do not want to issue a document that the whole world will see must be inoperative, like the Pope's bull against the comet. Would my word free the slaves when I cannot even enforce the Constitution in the rebel States?

Mr. Lincoln was in great straits; the border States, and the party more or less in sympathy with them, were pressing him for pledges that slavery should not be interfered with; the "Greeley faction" of the Republican party were urging immediate emancipation. President Welling says—and it shows us Mr. Lincoln's agony:

> It is true that only a few days previously, [to the meeting with the Chicago preachers,] 'when the rebel army was at Frederick,' [September 6,] he had registered a vow in heaven that he would issue a proclamation of emancipation so soon as the Confederates should be driven out of Maryland; but this was the conduct of a man who, in a perplexing state of incertitude, resolves his doubts by 'throwing a lot in the lap,' and leaving 'the whole disposing thereof to be of the Lord;' or, as I prefer to believe, it was that prudent and reverent waiting on Providence by which the President sought to guard against the danger of identifying the Proclamation in the popular mind with a panic cry of despair—in which latter case the hesitation of Mr. Lincoln only serves to set in a stronger light the significant fact that other than considerations of military necessity were held to dominate the situation; for, if they alone had been prevalent, the Proclamation could never have come more appropriately than when the military need was greatest.

The Proclamation was not simply, "a war measure," but "a political measure"; it was absolutely necessary to Mr. Lincoln to satisfy that element of his party that Mr. Greeley fairly represented in order to carry on the war at all. For its interest and importance I make another and longer extract from President Welling's article:

> The proximate and procuring cause of the Proclamation, as I conceive, is not far to seek. It was issued primarily and chiefly as a political necessity, and took on the character of a military necessity only because the President had been brought to believe that if he did not keep the radical portion of his party at his back he could not long be sure of keeping an army at the front. He had begun the conduct of the war on the theory that it was waged for the restoration of the Union under the Constitution, as it was at the outbreak of the secession movement. He sedulously labored to keep the war in this line of direction. He publicly deprecated

its degeneration into a remorseless revolutionary struggle. He cultivated every available alliance with the Union men of the border States. He sympathized with them in their loyalty, and in the political theory on which it was based. But the most active and energetic wing of the Republican party had become, as the war waxed hotter, more and more hostile to this 'border-State theory of the war,' until, in the end, its fiery and impetuous leaders did not hesitate to threaten him with repudiation as a political chief, and even began in some cases to hint the expediency of withholding supplies for the prosecution of the war, unless the President should remove "pro-slavery generals" from the command of our armies, and adopt an avowedly antislavery policy in the future conduct of the war. Thus placed between two stools, and liable between them to fall to the ground, he determined at last to plant himself firmly on the stool which promised the surest and safest support.

I am able to state with confidence that Mr. Lincoln gave this explanation of his changed policy a few days after the Preliminary Proclamation of September 22 had been issued. The Hon. Edward Stanly, the Military Governor of North Carolina, immediately on receiving a copy of that paper, hastened to Washington for the purpose of seeking an authentic and candid explanation of the grounds on which Lincoln had based such a sudden and grave departure from the previous theory of the war. Mr. Stanly had accepted the post of Military Governor of North Carolina at a great personal sacrifice, and with the distinct understanding that the war was to be conducted on the same constitutional theory which had presided over its inception by the Federal Government, and hence the proclamation not only took him by surprise, but seemed to him an act of perfidy. In this view he hastily abandoned his post, and came to throw up his commission and return to California, where he had previously resided. Before doing so he sought an audience with the President—in fact, held several interviews with him—on the subject; and knowing that, as a public journalist, I was deeply interested in the matter, he came to report to me the substance of the President's communications. That substance was recorded in my diary as follows:

"September 27. Had a call to-day at the 'Intelligencer' office from the Hon. Edward Stanly, Military Governor of North Carolina. In a long and interesting conversation Mr. Stanly related to me the substance of several interviews which he had with the President respecting the Proclamation of Freedom. Mr. Stanly said that the President had stated to him that the Proclamation had become a civil necessity to prevent the radicals from openly embarrassing the government in the conduct of the war. The President expressed the belief that, without the Proclamation for which they had been clamoring, the radicals would take the extreme step in Congress of withholding supplies for carrying on the war, leaving the whole land in anarchy. Mr. Lincoln said that he had prayed to the Almighty to save him from this necessity, adopting the very language of our Saviour, 'If it be possible, let this cup pass from me;' but the prayer had not been answered."

Of the Preliminary, or warning, Proclamation of September, 1862, the following is the important portion:

That on the first day of January, in the year of our Lord one thousand eight hundred and sixty-three, all persons held as slaves within any States, or designated parts of a State, the people whereof shall then be in rebellion against the United States, shall be then, thenceforward, and forever free; and the Executive Government of the United States, including the military and naval authority thereof, will recognize and maintain the freedom of such persons, and will do no act or acts to repress such persons, or any of them, in any efforts they may make for their actual freedom.

That the Executive will, on the first day of January aforesaid, by proclamation, designate the States and parts of States, if any, in which the people thereof respectively shall then be in rebellion against the United States; and the fact that any State, or the people thereof, shall on that day be in good faith represented in the Congress of the United States by members chosen thereto at elections wherein a majority of the qualified voters of such State shall have participated, shall, in the absence of strong countervailing testimony, be deemed conclusive evidence that such States, and the people thereof, are not then in rebellion against the United States.

What if the Confederate leaders had given up their struggle before January 1, 1863?

January 1, 1863, Mr. Lincoln issued the Proclamation, declaring all slaves as free in certain States, and parts of States, which he designated, as he had set forth in the warning of September 22, 1862.

This Proclamation did not touch such States as Maryland and Kentucky. The slaves in the other Southern States were practically set free as the Union armies advanced, conquering the country. But emancipation needed more than the President's Proclamation, as he had said before it was issued, and as he showed afterward in urging an amendment to the Constitution, forever abolishing and prohibiting slavery in the United States.

Mr. Dana, who was the devoted friend and the earnest champion of Mr. Lincoln through all the "storm and stress" of those eventful days, states the truth of the case in his review of President Welling's paper: "No doubt the proclamation of January 1, 1863, though such were not its terms, brought about a system of progressive military emancipation, taking effect as we advanced. But for the prohibition of slavery thereafter in the conquered States, under their Constitutions, as well as in the loyal States, very different action was required. The abolition of the slave system, as it stood in the Constitutions of so many States, was beyond the reach of the military power of the President, or of Congress. It called for the ultimate, sovereign legislative action of 'we, the people of the United States,' in the form of an amendment to the Constitution; and this, when adopted, precluded all question as to attempted past emancipation or abolition by proclamation."

No man knew better than Mr. Lincoln that his Proclamation did not secure freedom to the slaves. On this point President Welling says: "With a candor which did him honor he made no pretense of concealing its manifold infirmities either from his own eyes, or from the eyes of the people, so soon as Congress proposed, in a way of undoubted constitutionality and of undoubted efficacy, to put an end to slavery every-where in the Union by an amendment to the Constitution. Remarking on that amendment at the time of its proposal, he said, [President Welling here quotes Raymond's "Life and State Papers of Abraham Lincoln:"]

'A question might be raised as to whether the Proclamation was legally valid. It might be added that it aided only those who came into our lines, and that it was inoperative as to those who did not give themselves up; or that it would have no effect upon the children of those born hereafter; in fact, it could be urged that it did not meet the evil. But this amendment is a king's cure for all evils; it winds the whole thing up."

The negro's title to freedom does not rest in Mr. Lincoln's Proclamation, but in the Amendment to the Constitution of the United States. No doubt the "logic of events," the triumph of the Union armies, and the complete and final overthrow of the Confederate Government, gave tremendous potency to Mr. Lincoln's Proclamation; but the negro's right to his freedom is found in the amendments to the Constitution of the United States, which were first adopted by Congress, and made complete by the ratification of the several States.

This is the language of the "amendment" which gives legality to the negro's freedom, and guarantees it to him and to his children forever:

ARTICLE XIII

Section 1. Neither slavery nor involuntary servitude, except as a punishment for crime, whereof the party shall have been duly convicted, shall exist within the United States, or any place subject to their jurisdiction.

Section 2. Congress shall have power to enforce this article by appropriate legislation.

Whether the human instruments, used by God's providence to effect the emancipation of the negroes, were wise or just in their methods, I do not discuss. Best or worst, it was done in this way, and it is done forever. That Mr. Lincoln was truly opposed to slavery I do not doubt; that his Proclamation received the approval of the majority of the Christian world, I do not doubt; that the fact of emancipation—if not the mode—now receives the approval of those whom it made poor for a time, I do not doubt. Whatever may have been the secret thoughts and struggles of Mr.

Lincoln's mind; however his Proclamation may have been precipitated by the exigencies of a colossal war and by the urgency of the most vigorous section of the party that put him in power; however emancipation might have been delayed had the great question in dispute of battle been compromised while the war was still in progress; however pleasing Mr. Lincoln's course may have been to the majority of the Northern people; and however displeasing it may have been to the Southern people, this much at least is clear, the slaves are all free, and their freedom is recognized by all men every-where. And to me it is unthinkable that the providence of God, overruling all things—the good and the evil, the wise and the unwise methods and purposes of men on both sides of the contest—did not give freedom to the slaves, for their own good, for the good of the white race, for the good of two continents, and for the glory of his Son, Jesus Christ, the Saviour of men.

8

THE FREEDMAN MADE A CITIZEN

The emancipated negroes are citizens. They were made citizens by amendments to the Constitution of the United States. The amendments were ordained by the conjoined action of Congress and of a sufficient number of States to meet the constitutional requirement in such a case.

The vital points in these amendments, so far as the negro's citizenship is concerned, are found in the Fourteenth and Fifteenth Amendments. The Fourteenth reads:

Section 1. All persons born or naturalized in the United States, and subject to the jurisdiction thereof, are citizens of the United States and of the State wherein they reside. No State shall make or enforce any law which shall abridge the privileges or immunities of citizens of the United States; nor shall any State deprive any person of life, liberty, or property, without due process of law, nor deny to any person within its jurisdiction the equal protection of the laws.

The Fifteenth Amendment reads:

Section 1. The right of citizens of the United States to vote shall not be denied or abridged by the United States or any State on account of race, color, or previous condition of servitude.

Section 2. The Congress shall have power to enforce this article by appropriate legislation."

The negroes are not only citizens in that they are entitled to complete protection under the laws in all their rights of person and property, but also citizens in that all males, twenty-one years old, not disqualified by crime or other conditions that would disqualify a white man, are entitled to vote. Every negro man of lawful age, if otherwise qualified, has the same legal right to vote that the President of the United States has.

It is now practically too late, in this country, to argue the advantages or disadvantages of universal suffrage. Much has been said for and against the doctrine of universal suffrage—"manhood suffrage," as the phrase is. But the time is past for such arguments; facts and not theories must be considered now. The people, acting through their representatives, some because they thought it wise, some as a means of political power, and others because they were obliged to do it, have adopted universal suffrage as a fundamental principle and have incorporated it into our entire political system. We must now make the best of it. After all, it may be best as it is; such matters are only determined by experiment; we are now making the test. Such experiments cannot be worked out in a year, or even in a generation. We know too little of such matters to dogmatize about them; after all the experience and wisdom of the past, what we call statesmanship is but a complicated, difficult, and uncertain experiment. But common sense teaches at least this much: when we cannot have what we prefer we should do the very best we can with what we have.

Whether the wholesale enfranchisement of the negro was a party measure, as his sudden and unconditioned emancipation was a war measure urged on by a political necessity; whether it was done in a paroxysm of feeling and sentimentalism; whether it was designed, in part at least, as a repression of any reactionary tendencies in the "old masters," we need not discuss at this time. When there is less noise of men running to and fro with dim lanterns or flaming torches in their hands; when there is less outcry and dissonance of fiercely contending passions; when there is less sensitiveness and prejudice, philosophical historians may discuss, with whatever ability and insight may be given to them, these difficult subjects that are now entangled in a hundred folds of warring interests and ambitions. But we must deal with the facts as we find them. A wise man who proposes to rebuild a burned house will not quarrel with his neighbors or workmen about the origin of the fire, nor exhaust his time and energies in fruitless lamentations over the unsuitableness of his materials. He cannot live with his family under the open sky, unless he proposes to be a savage. A house he must have; he will use his materials to the best possible advantage; if he cannot procure the best stone out of the quarries, he will use the best he has. If he can do no better he will build of sun-dried bricks, or of bricks that have twice known fire. Even an adobe house is better than none.

At this time the people of the South may read with profit the life and labors of Nehemiah. History does not record a fairer, truer patriotism than his. He gave up a pleasant and profitable office "in Shushan the palace" to rebuild Jerusalem, that had been laid waste in bitter wars and relentless sieges. There are few more pathetic passages in the lives of patriotic men than we see in Nehemiah when he "went out by night . . . and viewed the walls of Jerusalem, which were broken down, and the gates thereof were consumed with fire." For his great task of rebuilding the sacred city he had small resources and manifold discouragements. His friends were dispirited and unorganized; his enemies were strong, bold, scoffing. He had to build the new out of the ruins of the old city. When, after incredible exertions, he had rallied a small but united and determined company for the work of restoration, there was not lacking a Sanballat to mock their patriotic efforts. No doubt many of those Jews who held their brethren down under "mortgages and bondage," were more in sympathy with Sanballat than with Nehemiah. Which was harder for the brave and great-hearted patriot to bear, the jeers of his enemies or the apathy or secret hate of those who ought to have been his helpers, it would be hard to say. There were not lacking Jews who said, "O, you can't do any thing with the ruins of the old Jerusalem." As for Sanballat, this describes him, and not only him, but some of our own times who have for the struggling South only jeers and contempt:

But it came to pass, that when Sanballat heard that we builded
the wall, he was wroth, and took great indignation, and mocked
the Jews. And he spoke before his brethren and the army of Sa-
maria, and said, What do these feeble Jews? will they fortify
themselves? will they sacrifice? will they make an end in a day?
will they revive the stones out of the heaps of the rubbish which
are burned.

The South has heard this Sanballat voice many times since
Appomattox. And Sanballat has had to help him a class of Southern men, as greedy as vultures and as remorseless as death, who
have done nothing to rebuild our broken walls and our burned
gates, who have used their power and opportunity only to hold
faster the poor and the helpless of their own brethren. In this old
history there is one other character who still survives to play his
little part of imitation. There was one Tobiah, small echo of Sanballat, and this is the picture of him: "Now Tobiah the Ammonite
was by him, and he said, Even that which they build, if a fox go
up, he shall even break down their stone wall."

But Sanballat's prophecies came to naught, and Tobiah's mean
jests came back to him. Nehemiah and his patriotic band did rebuild Jerusalem, its walls and its gates. Let the men of the South
take courage, and out of the ruins of their old system and out of
the very difficulties of the new era, build up a better civilization
than they ever knew. They can if they will; "the eternal powers"
will help them.

Let us consider the difficulties of our position, as Nehemiah,
before he began to rebuild, surveyed the ruins of the city of his
fathers, recalling its vanished glories that he might strengthen his
heart for the work of restoration. We find ourselves face to face
with as difficult a problem as was ever committed to any people
of any age. Take any view possible of the history of the emancipation and enfranchisement of the negroes, and this portentous fact
remains: nearly a million of men, who had been slaves, were made
voters before they could read. They were told to vote upon the
most difficult and complicated of all questions, questions of public policy, involving the interests of half a continent and of nearly

fifty millions of people, before they could read or understand the Constitution under which they were governed.

Such an experiment was never made before by any people. There is something impressive in the very audacity of the measure, and in the greatness of the danger which it involves. Those who proposed and carried it through had either a sublime confidence in the government they put in jeopardy, or an amazing indifference to the dangers to which they exposed its institutions, or a great passion that blinded their eyes. Those who wonder that confusion came into our politics are not read in history; they are not wise in the knowledge of human nature. The wonder is not that disorders, corruptions, violence, followed the introduction of this new and strange element—this fearful combination of power and ignorance—but that utter chaos did not follow. It is, perhaps, not too much to say there was never any other government, there is not to-day any other government in the world, capable of enduring such a strain as the American people put upon their civil institutions between 1865 and 1870. Surely there is in the American system of government, there is in this Republic of ours, a vitality never manifested by any other system in any nation or time.

What is the explanation of this, the most wonderful fact in our history—the fact that placing the ballot in the hands of nearly a million of men, of all others the least qualified to perform this high function of citizenship, has not before this time destroyed the Republic? And what reasons have we for the hope that our institutions may continue to survive such trials of their stability? Statesmen and philosophers can, no doubt, give us learned and profound answers. There are some that will occur to plain people who reflect on these subjects: 1. Ours is a new country; it offers large opportunity, outside of politics, for the expenditure of restless energy. 2. The American people are, as a class, intensely practical. They are not swept away by a craze. Emotional revolutions, like some that have occurred in France, are impossible in this country. 3. The form and genius of our government make it capable of vast adjustability. 4. The preponderance of Christian principle and sentiment has done more to save us than any other characteristic of our people or government. 5. Above all, the providence of God.

Whether the next generation shall witness the continuance of good government depends largely upon a condition not now satisfied, namely, the education of these untaught voters. (I do not forget the great and sore need of the education of all white voters, also, wherever found.) If we of today take the matter in kind as we ought, and teach these new citizens and voters all that we can teach them of their duties, and prepare them for their performance as well as can prepare them, our children will "rise up and call us blessed." But is it irreverent to ask, Whether we may rely upon divine Providence to continue to bless us if we are unfaithful to the plain duties that are pressing upon us? Providence blesses the use of right means to good ends.

The fact that the emancipated negro was a voter, and that practically his vote was not his own, made the struggle hard for the new citizen from 1865 to 1880. It will never be, in some respects, at least, so hard for him again, unless there is unexampled stupidity somewhere. For now his vote is sought in the South. It has been divided once, in some States, at least. Henceforth it will be divided many times; it is almost certain that it will never be "solid" again. It may be, in some localities, better for the new citizen's personal safety; perhaps it will be worse for his morals. Wise men will see danger here; would that they knew how to meet it!

Free man and citizen our colored brother is, and so he will remain. He will never be re-enslaved; he will never be disfranchised. It may come about some day that the South will be exceedingly zealous in defending his right to vote, and that the North will realize, in ways not agreeable, the tremendous power of the black man's ballot. The time may come when the North will have sore need of patience with this voter, as the South has had sore need for these years. Will the North be wiser or more patient? They think so. May they not be disappointed in themselves! May great grace be given to our brethren of the North when the trial of their faith comes! They will need it as the South has needed it.

This vote will be "counted"; the North may depend on this.

There may, for a long time, or for all time, be local exceptions, as there may be, and as there have been, exceptions in New York, and in other great cities; but, in the long run, and as a rule, the black man's vote will be counted. On this point our Northern friends may dismiss their fears. What they say ought to be done the Southern whites will soon say must be done. While I am writing this chapter an active canvass is going on in my own county, Newton, for county officers. Our men are patriotic and willing to serve their country in office. There is no lack of candidates; I suppose there never will be. All told, there must be more than twenty men interested in the result. Parties are confusedly mixed. The candidate for Clerk of the County Court has no opposition, and he is the leading Republican in the county. One of the candidates for sheriff was in the old days a slave-holder, and he will secure the largest negro vote, although he is rated as a "stalwart" Democrat.[1] All these candidates are courting the negro vote. In their eyes, as to this election at least, "a negro is as good as a white man," if not somewhat better. Nothing is more certain than that every negro vote deposited in Covington and at other precincts in this county, day after to-morrow, January 5, 1881, will be counted. And on that day the negro vote will be courted and divided and counted all over Georgia.

North and South, those who are jealous of the purity of the ballot-box will, in the management of the intricate and difficult questions involved in our elections, need all the sense and virtue and patience and courage that are in them.

---

[1] He was elected, the majoriy of negroes voting for him, as was anticipated.

9

THE TIME ELEMENT IN THIS PROBLEM

To my purpose, not to discuss "dead issues" here or elsewhere, I adhere. If history feels obliged to exhume the dead, let those do the work who find pleasure in it. But to know what the living issues are, to get fairly hold of the problems of to-day and of to-morrow—for our children's children will not see the end of it—it is needful to look back a little at events since the war.

Of all parties, especially of two, the Northern and the Southern whites, some things should be said in perfect good temper and fairness.

First of all, to go no further back, there has been, since April, 1865, a great folly and a great heat on both sides. The North has gone too fast, the South too slow. The conquerors have been impatient, after the manner of conquerors; the conquered have been sore under their yoke, and reluctant to "accept the situation," after the manner of conquered people. Sometimes, when it would have been wiser to have pulled up the steep hill the heavy loads put upon us, we have pulled rather against both "yoke and bows," hurting our galled and bleeding necks all the more. Power, riches, "fullness of bread" in the North have not ministered to forbearance and patience; overthrow, poverty, want, and the constant pressure and menace of power have not ministered to political or other resignation in the South. Moreover, Northern impatience has very largely increased Southern reluctance.

Our Northern fellow-citizens never put themselves in our

place. I cannot blame them; they could not. It is a feat impossible even to imagination. But they could at least have made the attempt with more painstaking care. If the relations of the two sections to slavery and the other questions in dispute had been the same, they should remember the differences between victory and defeat. And as they conquered us "for the Union," the obligations of magnanimous patience are all the greater; we were not a foreign nation; three to one they conquered their brothers.

One night, in Atlanta, Georgia, toward the close of the war, I heard an eccentric old Frenchman, Dr. D'Alvigney, a surgeon in the Confederate Army, make a speech to a meeting of citizens at the City Hall. It was brief, but pointed, and easy to remember. His introduction was personal; a few nights before he had "veree bad luck." "The storm," he said, "blew down the buggy house, and smashed my buggy, somebody stole my horse, and my cow runned away." He had our sympathies at once. The old doctor then proceeded to tell us why it was necessary for us to succeed in the struggle. He had known war and political convulsion in France. This was his peroration:

"Fellow-citizens, I have been in two revolutions before this. One time I was conquer-er, one time I was the conquer-ed. I tell you dere is one great deeferance in dose two leetle lettare."

No doubt the game old Frenchman was right; we know the "d," the North knows the "r." If they could put themselves on the other side, only in imagination, and only for a moment, (I have not the heart to ask it longer,) they would recall many words they have spoken, and undo some things that they have done. I am willing to apply the doctrine of repentance fairly; a philosopher on the "conquered" side should make allowance, considering the weakness of our nature, for even the pride and impatience of conquerors. Although not a philosopher, I am doing my best.

There are differences in the circumstances of the two parties, not merely in the issues of the struggle, but in their past relations to the matters in dispute. Slavery ceased in the Northern States (unless I should except the few hundred negroes who were held in bondage in the orderly and excellent State of Connecticut till

1840—poor, lonesome creatures that they were) before any of the present generation were born. The people of the South had never known the negro except as a slave. When Northern slave-holders let go their grip on the negroes there were so few that their influence was inconsiderable. When Southern slaves were set free and made citizens, many thousands of white men being, for a time, disfranchised, they were strong enough in numbers and outside help to control things.

Our Northern friends will think better of us—at least less of themselves—in this matter if they will read their own history. Most of them seem to have forgotten that there are men still living who have been mobbed in Northern cities for preaching abolitionism. The cause of African freedom had its martyrs in the North, also. These facts they should call to mind in justice to their dead and to our living. Their present attitude on this question they did not reach at a bound. Let Greeley, Garrison, and the rest tell how they struggled through the life-time of a generation, and how slowly the mass of the people rallied about them. Let them call up the records of elections a generation gone, and count the votes they gave to presidential candidates, braving the world and certain defeat on this question of negro slavery. Let it be remembered, also, that it was not simply the force of what they believed to be the pure truth of God on this question, but the firing on Fort Sumter and "the old flag" that made the millions of the North practically "solid" for abolitionism in 1861.

Forgetting these things in their own history, as well as overlooking the relations of the South to the subject, the mass of the Northern people have judged us hardly and harshly. They have often been censorious an impatient because the South which had owned slaves from the beginning, and had just lost them after a bloody and disastrous war, was not "born in a day!" Forgetting their own history as to the evolution, through two or three generations, of their advanced views, they have been impatient that the South should, not only formally, by solemn constitutional enactments, accept the negro as a freeman and a voter, but heartily fall in love with the new system that, in every Southern State that had gone fully into the war, put the government in the hands of strangers and of the slaves of yesterday, disfranchised thousands of the former leaders and rulers of the people, and left them nothing to do with government except the burden of new and heavy taxation. All this was "a weariness to the flesh," but not so exasperating as were the demands of certain *doctrinaires*, more zealous than wise, who strenuously insisted that the South should accept the "advanced views" as well as the "new facts."

Some of the absurdest things in the world were talked by these zealots. For instance, in 1867, in a crowded car, a Federal judge said to me, "You people must accept emancipation, negro suffrage, social equality, amalgamation, and all." My answer was: "Judge, I beg of you to leave out the coloring matter." He hardly forgave me for the laugh which followed at his expense; some of his hearers, brooding over their troubles, and suspicious of troubles yet to come, and not well enough acquainted with the "wild" judge to appreciate his exquisite absurdities, never forgave him at all. Some may say, "People were very silly to care for such absurd speeches." Very true; but what of the United States judge, backed by "the troops," who could so far forget himself as to say such things? Such absurdities as the judge's talk amused a few, disgusted many, startled and alarmed hundreds and thousands all over the South. People could not tell how far the new ideas might be pressed.

Many little occurrences in every community where the troops were quartered added to the wide-spread feeling of distrust and alarm. One of the least irritating I mention. It will suggest to sensible people some of the difficulties in the way of our "regeneration" of opinion and feeling on this whole question. As if one should collar with a strong hand a sinner truly "convicted," drag him to the altar, force him upon his knees, beat him as well as lecture him for his sins, and yet expect him to be "converted" within the hour! One day, in the autumn of 1865, I was superintending the erection, out of the *débris* of a torn-down house, of a little cottage on Crew-street, Atlanta. Three or four negro men were at work, one of them being a carpenter. While we were busy at work one morning, a very young lieutenant, commanding a small squad of soldiers, drew up on the sidewalk. The lieutenant, drawn sword in hand, without so much as saying, "Good morning," demanded of me, "Are you carrying on this work?" I answered, "Yes, sir." "What do you pay these men?" I confess that he did not appear lovely in my eyes, but I did not want to have my work stopped while being marched to "headquarters." So, with all the meekness possible to me, I answered, "I pay the carpenter $3 a day, the laborers $1 50." His serene highness "approved" me, and marched on to inquire into other people's business. I understood well enough that his superiors were intent on preventing us from "cheating the negroes." It did not seem to occur to them that we would hardly be silly enough to do this, even granting that we were thieves, seeing that there was not enough labor in Atlanta to meet the constant demand.

Every Southern man knows that my illustration of our "temptations to fret" is taken from the mildest of our experiences. Most farmers in 1865 could give an "experience."

It was a Dutchman who flogged his son for cursing; then flogged him for crying; then flogged him for silence, resenting that as sullenness. Rod in hand, he fell upon his son the third time, saying, "Hans, you dinks cuss; I flogs you for dat." This administrator of "paternal government" was not wise—to stop at wisdom. If "Hans" had no more grace than his father had sense it is much to be feared that he did curse after the third flogging.

I have no disposition to set in order the facts and experiences of the "Reconstruction Period." This I may say: in those days a degree of divine grace was needed by Southern people not often experienced in this sinful world. And if those days had not been shortened—

Living in Atlanta during that chaotic time, and knowing that I was seeing with my eyes and hearing with my ears a most unique chapter in our national history, that could never be written, I attended almost constantly the sessions of the "Conventions" and "Legislatures" held in that city under military authority, and that which immediately succeeded it. Those assemblies were never matched outside the "conquered territory." Looking back at these times, in the calm of this winter night—I give it as my solemn judgment—great grace was given to the Southern people. I grant that they did not "live up to their privileges." But candor will say, if the South failed in patient submission, the North failed in wise forbearance.

Is it any wonder that the great caldron boiled fiercely, and that it sometimes boiled over?

At this point a delicate subject needs some consideration. The present difficulties of our hard and tangled race-problem cannot be understood or mastered without some knowledge of the blunders, follies, and sins of both sides, as connected with various enterprises set on foot in the North, and designed to teach and to evangelize the negroes.

No doubt the various missionary and educational societies that, soon after the war closed, moved down upon the South, had, at bottom, a good impulse and a good spirit. These enterprises were backed by the brains, money, and prayers of some of the best people who ever lived. Of this I never had a moment's doubt. Moreover, many of the men and women who came South to teach and to preach were among the saints of the earth.

But all saints are not wise, and some who were not saints "came also among them." (See Job 1.6.) It would have been a marvel indeed, if, among so many, some impostors had not thrust themselves, making a "gain of godliness," pushing their fortunes, and watching their chances in the conquered provinces, as did the hangers-on who went out with Roman consuls to see what spoils they could win. A few wild people, not generally of the teaching and preaching company, I must believe, swept away by fanaticism, told the negroes that their labor had made the wealth of the South, and that they were entitled to divide it. I myself heard one preacher use language the most inflammatory, before a crowd of excited negroes, a few months after the Southern surrender, at a Sunday evening meeting in one of their churches, about the parallels between the bondage of the children of Israel in Egypt and Southern slavery. I will never forget the frenzy in his eyes, and the hoarse passion in his voice, when he dwelt upon the "spoiling of the Egyptians" by the departing Hebrews. I believe the man really thought that the freed people were entitled to divide, on a pretty communistic basis, with their ex-masters. I am sure the missionary society he represented never indulged such madness; but how could the mass of Southern people know the real inspiration of a movement that, by some unlucky accident, had made a spokesman and representative of this man? One such man was enough to excite prejudice, unrelenting and invincible, against a dozen men of sense and genuine missionary zeal. This man was thoroughly "ostracised"; that is, every Southern man suspected him of being an incendiary, and no Southern man would have any thing to do with him when it was possible to avoid him.

Some of the most zealous and devoted greatly lacked in common prudence. Some had a fierce and hot zeal that was near akin to fanaticism, Some acted as no missionary in any land ever acted and succeeded in doing good. More than once I have heard harangues to excited negroes that would have issued in fire and blood but for the religious teaching and training they had received from Southern preachers long before 1861. As I wish to state things exactly as I believe them to have been, I will add to this—and but for their fear of the Southern man's vengeance. Now and then some appalling outrage, followed by appalling vengeance, would occur. Justly or unjustly, it was not unnatural, in the excitements, passions, and prejudices of such a time, that outrages by negroes, as rape and arson, were, in many instances, in popular suspicion, connected with the teaching and influence of people, some, at least, of whose representatives were capable of making such speeches as have been mentioned above. This may have been an unjust suspicion in every instance; it certainly was in nearly every case. But it was not unnatural that all connected with these enterprises were, at the beginning, more or less thrown into false positions, in the judgment of Southern people by the arrant folly and madness of a few; for the simple reason that these wild fanatics were very soon known to and by our people—they were noisy, voluble, self-assertive, obtrusive; while those who really did what they were sent to do were quiet, and, confining their labors to their teaching and their preaching, were, for a long time, unknown to their Southern neighbors. It was natural and inevitable that there should, for a long time, be little communication between the "missionaries" and the Southern whites. And a few of us who tried to know something of the better ones were, ever and anon, given to understand that we had "never done any real good Christian work" in these States, and the result was—we were "discouraged with them."

I grant that we of the South were over-suspicious; but this weakness of our common humanity we shared with the people of the North. There were differences in our suspicions, it may be; ours the suspicions natural to the defeated, theirs the suspicions natural to the victorious. As to this matter neither side has shown any great superiority of temper or penetration. North and South, we may well afford to strike a fair balance with mutual confessions, apologies, and amendments.

Since January 1, 1881, I have been seriously asked by one of the most cultivated, liberal, and best known of Northern men "whether it is really true that Southern women, as a class, teach their children to hate Yankees." He knew better, but he told me that thousands of people, all over the North, believe it. Why? Because some foolish man, as a sort of last shriek of baffled passion, in some absurd speech had said as much! I told him, "No, sir; I have never seen nor heard of a Southern woman doing so wicked a thing." It would be as wise in the South to believe that the wild and rattle-brained Federal judge who declared to me in the presence of a large company that "the South must accept amalgamation," represented the constant thought, fixed purpose; and intense longing of every Northern man and woman.

Among sane people, capable of attending to the the ordinary business affairs of every-day life, this sort of folly should have an end; common sense, as well as Christian charity, may make large allowance for the waves that continued to roll over us all, long after the furious tempests of a four years' war had spent their force. But even the waves sink to rest at last. Will Christian men and women never hear the voice of their Lord and Christ, saying, "Peace, be still?"

I mention the case of one man in a prominent and important position. With my own eyes I saw him (he was a teacher employed by one of the missionary associations) soon after his appearance in a Southern city, work all day—a detachment of United States troops being on the ground—persuading the recently enfranchised negroes to vote down the ticket that represented nearly all the intelligence and property of that city, and against the men who, under any administration, had to bear the expenses of government, even the relief of the sick and indigent of the very people who were arrayed against them. The legal right of this zealous man to do such things is not in question; but his course was exasperating. To say the least of it, it did not commend his "mission" to those whose influence could have greatly helped him to fulfill it. Such conduct would, I suspect, have been a trial of faith and love in Boston itself. It is not impossible that the spirited young men of that city would, but for the bayonets; have pitched him into the bay, after the tea-chests of 1774.

Long ago this teacher has learned his business after a better method and spirit. He would not, with his experience, repeat his unwise and unnecessary provocations. Long ago the men who, at the beginning, "ostracised" him, that is, let him alone, have recognized his true worth, and have given him what help they could.

But there were not a few like this over-zealous man; he was young then, and mightily persuaded that he was right, and ready to follow his "views," even to martyrdom. He seemed to long for it. Thank Heaven! he missed his crown. As much politician as preacher, as much partisan as teacher, and known to the people only in his most unlovely and undesirable characters, it is not surprising that he did not, at first, command either the confidence or co-operation of those who, from their stand-point and from their knowledge, could only look upon him as an enemy and a dangerous man.

Such mistaken people did incalculable harm. And as most of them were ready writers, they gave their "experience"—omitting ours—to the Northern press from week to week. For example, the teacher whose performances I have mentioned told the world how he was "ostracised," but omitted to tell how he had left his teaching for the conflicts of the hustings. When they came to make up their Southern letters for Northern papers they added to their own experience whatever they could hear from others. So it came to pass that the whole South was covered by a corps of volunteer "reporters" to the Northern press, both secular and religious. Many of them were "writing up a line of things," as a distinguished minister called it in an interview I had with him in Cincinnati, in May, 1880; and all our worst points, and I grant that there were and are many, went into their letters. Alas! our better points, and I am sure we have many, were left out. Nor could these people comprehend, at first, the problem they were dealing with. These letters, or extracts from them, sometimes garbled, found their way back to the Southern press. The Southern press answered with just denunciation of those who misrepresented us, and very often with unjust denunciation of a whole class. The Northern press replied with fresh reports; the Southern press rejoined with an array of Northern criminal statistics. They said, "You are a nation of cut-throats"; we pointed to the appalling number of divorces in some Northern States, and said, "You are a nation of adulterers." And thus for fifteen mortal years we have gone on throwing mud at each other, to the wrath of God, the disgust of good men, and the delight of the devil.

I do not say, I have never said, the Southern people came out of their "fiery furnace" without the "smell of fire upon their garments." It is easy to say they ought to have seen the humble preacher in the ardent politician, the devoted teacher in the fierce partisan. Perhaps. But it was not in human nature, in the South or anywhere else.

Frankly I admit that Southern people as a class—I bear my part of the blame—did their cause much damage by themselves taking extreme positions. For example, I chanced to know a cultivated and pious New England woman, Miss ———, who came to a Southern village to teach a negro school. As I became well acquainted with her I respected and admired her. I showed her what kindness I could. She bore herself admirably in a most trying position. She made few mistakes, and never showed a bad spirit. But the community never knew her; she received no social recognition, except the commonest courtesies. She received no hurt; she was simply let alone. Could she have remained longer she would have won confidence and love, for she deserved both. I do not defend the coldness and suspicion of these villagers toward this lovely New England lady, but they should not be hastily denounced as utterly lost to "chivalry" or charity by those who can never know how much reason they had to suspect the spirit and fear the influence of many who came on such errands.

The impatient, the censorious, the partisan people who got themselves mixed up with these missionary movements southward—especially the "ready writers" who rushed into print to tell all the bad that was in us, and who, from their stand-point and in their light, could never see our better characteristics—shut, for years, most doors against the whole class.

Let both sides look calmly at these facts; it is time to cool off and recognize the truth of things. Was it not inevitable, human nature being what it is, that many persons should come South after the war, consumed with zeal to do good, to lift up the ignorant and degraded, but, by their constitution, unfitted to work in such a field at such a time, and by their methods doomed to failure? Was it not equally inevitable that what has been properly enough called "ostracism" should soon manifest itself—shutting them out from the houses of many people who thought them bad and dangerous? Was it not inevitable that those who in nowise deserved "ostracism" suffered what some undoubtedly did deserve? Was it not inevitable that there should be mistakes, misjudgments, and heart-burnings on both sides? When wiser people came there was good sense and relenting on both sides, and the worst is now over.

But, after all, does history record an example, in any race or age, where a people of strong character went so far in fifteen years as the Southern people—a race of Anglo-Saxon blood—have gone since 1865 in the modification of opinions, in the change of sentiments that had been, through generations, firmly fixed in all their thinking and feeling? The change in the opinions and sentiments of the Southern people since 1865 is one of the most wonderful facts of history. It far surpasses the remarkable material recuperation of the South after complete overthrow, and what, at the time, seemed to be remediless disaster. Had the South made more rapid progress in adopting the ideas of the New Era the world might well have doubted her sincerity.

One of the overlooked but most needful lessons for both the North and the South is this: in many processes of development the *time-element* is a condition absolute. Some processes require a great deal of time. In many cases we are most impatient of delay when delay is most essential. The general analogy of nature is that the finest growths are slowest. Nature will not be greatly hurried. Vegetable growths may be hastened by skillful treatment, but no hot-house devices can create even Jonah's gourd in an hour or a day. A lady friend of mine killed her geraniums by forcing them overmuch. Time is an essential condition in the growth of most opinions, and of all the established sentiments. There is a class of opinions that may be changed without violence upon the instant of receiving new evidence. A man on a journey will change his route upon receiving new information. An opinion about the rights and wrongs of things that is "bred in the bone" can hardly be changed on the instant of hearing new argument. If the new view be the truth, its seed must germinate and grow till it displaces the old. Opinions that are rooted in race-sentiments cannot be changed to order, under any logic or any pressure whatever. But time and the silent power of the "leaven" of truth does wonders—sometimes works miracles. If the South was as civilized in 1865 as her warmest champions and eulogists declared her to be, she could not reverse her cultured sentiments in a day; if she was as ignorant and barbarous as her harshest critics affirmed that she was, she had at least to learn their wisdom before she could imitate their example or emulate their graces. In any case *time* was as needful as the light of knowledge, and far more needful than the pressure of power.

If any suppose that I have written this chapter or this book to defend any real fault or real wrong with which the South is justly chargeable, he is mistaken. This is neither a confession nor a defense; I desire only to state facts and truths as they appear to me. And feeling profoundly that the people of the United States, and not of any one section only, have a vast and difficult race-problem to solve, I seek, by such means as I can command, to help forward, to the best of my ability, a somewhat better understanding between two greatly and sinfully estranged sections of our common country, that they may be persuaded and helped, in some measure, to co-operate with each other in a difficult and important task where, without co-operation, failure is inevitable. And now, in closing this chapter, I desire to record the opinion that, of all others, the worst misfortune that has befallen the South, in the long train of her disasters, is this painful and unmistakable fact: The spirit of censoriousness and suspicion, of criticism and disparagement, of complaint and denunciation, that has so long, so often, and so insistently shown itself in many Northern papers, on many Northern platforms, and in many Northern pulpits, has greatly hindered the South from coming to a knowledge of her own faults. It is an unspeakably sadder thing, and in every way more harmful, that a man should be blind to his own faults than that others should condemn him unjustly. And sadder, because blindness to our own faults prevents conviction, hinders repentance, and precludes reformation. But great is his triumph, who, being unjustly condemned in many things, is yet wise and brave enough to discover his faults and amend his ways.

The question for a true man to ask is, Not whether I have been accused unjustly in one thing or many, but whether I have done wrong in anything. Not whether I have in one thing or many been treated unjustly, but whether I have deserved censure in any thing. Not whether by human judgment I have been condemned unjustly in one thing or many, but whether I am condemned by the divine judgment in any thing. If we ask these questions with an honest heart we will find our answer. An honest heart, searching itself, will verify that word of our Lord: "If therefore thine eye be single, thy whole body shall be full of light." And it is a light that will lead men out of all darkness into the "true Light, which lighteth every man that cometh into the world."

10

CANTERBURY GREEN IN 1831–1884

At this place let us read an editorial, taken from "Scribner's Magazine" for December, 1880. It is presumably from the pen of Dr. J. G. Holland. I reproduce it here simply because it is, at this time, useful reading for both sides. Let Northern people take counsel of recent history in one of their best States, and learn—several things. Let Southern people read this ugly chapter, and consider that the conduct of the people of Canterbury Green would be just as infamous if perpetrated in a Southern village. Sometimes observant persons break off ridiculous or offensive habits when they see them in other people. If any of us have, at any time or in any way, been unjust, even in our opinions, to those who were trying to do the negro good—and some of us, I for one, have been unjust at times and to some—let this Connecticut case open our eyes. Never did the maltreatment of a negro, or of a negro teacher, appear more hideous to me than in reading this case—Connecticut case I might say, since the Legislature rallied to the help of the town meeting. And this occurred only twenty-seven years before the struggle began that was to drench this land in the blood of brothers. The Canterbury trouble involved, alas! the Congregational Church in the little village. Only twenty-seven years! No doubt there are men and women now living about Canterbury Green who took part in the persecution of brave Miss Crandall. Possibly some of the boys who behaved so unchivalrously toward her helped right manfully to conquer us of the South into the views they now entertain.

When our Northern friends read this history, and others like it, then, before they pronounce judgment upon their Southern brethren, let them first read what St. Paul says in his Epistle to the Galatians: "Brethren, if a man be overtaken in a fault, ye which are spiritual, restore such a one in the spirit of meekness; considering thyself, lest thou also be tempted."

May this Canterbury Green history help Northern critics of the South to be more moderate and charitable. May it also lead both sides to repentance.

The December "Scribner," in "Topics of the Time," says:

> We have a lesson at hand which may perhaps give our Northern people a charitable view of the Southern sentiment, and inspire them with hope of a great and radical change. We draw this from a work recently issued by the author, Miss Ellen D. Larned, which seems to be a careful, candid, and competent history of Windham County, Connecticut. It appears that, in 1831, Miss Prudence Crandall, a spirited, well known, and popular resident of the county, started a school for girls at Canterbury Green. The school was popular and was attended not only by girls from the best families in the immediate region, but by others from other counties and other States. Among these pupils she received a colored girl. She was at once told by the parents of the white children that the colored girl must be dismissed, or that their girls would be withdrawn from her establishment. Miss Crandall must have been a delightfully plucky woman, for she defied her patrons, sent all their children back to them, and advertised her school as a boarding-school for "young ladies and little misses of color." Of course the people felt themselves to be insulted, and they organized resistance. They appointed a committee of gentlemen to hold an interview with Miss Crandall and to remonstrate with her: But that sturdy person justified her course and stood by her scheme, as well she might. It was her business and it was none of theirs. The excitement in the town was without bounds. A town-meeting was hastily summoned "to devise and adopt such measures as would effectually avert the nuisance, or speedily abate it, if it should be brought into the village."

In 1833 Miss Crandall opened her school, against the protest of an indignant populace, who, after the usual habit of a Yankee town, called and held another town-meeting, at which it was resolved: "That the establishment or rendezvous falsely denominated a school, was designed by its projectors as the theater… to promulgate their disgusting doctrines of amalgamation and their pernicious sentiments of subverting the Union. These pupils were to have been congregated here from all quarters, tinder the false pretense of educating them, but really to scatter firebrands, arrows, and death among brethren of our own blood."

Let us remember that all this ridiculous disturbance was made about a dozen little darky girls, incapable of any seditious design, and impotent to do any sort of mischief. Against one of these little girls the people leveled an old vagrant law, requiring her to return to her home in Providence, or give security for her maintenance, on penalty of being "whipped on the naked body." At this time, as the author says,—

Canterbury did its best to make scholars and teachers uncomfortable. Non-intercourse and embargo acts were put in successful operation. Dealers in all sorts of wares and produce agreed to sell nothing to Miss Crandall, the stage-driver declined to carry her pupils, and neighbors refused a pail of fresh water, even though they knew that their own sons had filled her well with stable refuse. Boys and rowdies were allowed unchecked—if not openly encouraged—to exercise their utmost ingenuity in mischievous annoyance, throwing real stones and rotten eggs at the windows, and following the school with hoots and horns if it ventured to appear in the street.

Miss Crandall's Quaker father was threatened with mob violence, and was so terrified that he begged his daughter to yield to the demands of popular sentiment: but she was braver than he, and stood by herself and her school. Then Canterbury appealed to the Legislature, and did not appeal in vain. A statute, designed to meet the case, was enacted, which the inhabitants received with pealing bells and booming cannon, and "every demonstration of popular delight and triumph." This law was brought to bear upon Miss Crandall's father and mother, in the following choice note from two of their fellow-citizens:

"MR. CRANDALL: If you go to your daughter's, you are to be fined $100 for the first offense, $200 for the second, and double it every time. Mrs. Crandall, if you go there you will be fined, and your daughter Almira will be fined, and Mr. May, and those gentlemen from Providence, [Messrs. George and Henry Benson,] if they come here, will be fined at the same rate. And your daughter, the one that has established the school for colored females, will be taken up the same way as for stealing a horse, or for burglary. Her property will not be taken, but she will be put in jail, not having the liberty of the yard. There is no mercy to be shown about it."

Soon afterward, Miss Crandall was arrested and taken to jail. Her trial resulted in her release, but her establishment was persecuted by every ingenuity of cruel insult. She and her school were shut out from attendance at the Congregational Church, and religious services held in her own house were interrupted by volleys of rotten eggs and other missiles. The house was then set on fire. The fire was extinguished, and in 1834, on September 9, just as the family was going to bed, a body of men surrounded the house silently, and then, with iron bars, simultaneously beat in the windows. This, of course, was too much for the poor woman and girls. Miss Crandall herself quailed before this manifestation of ruffianly hatred, and the brave woman broke up her school and sent her pupils home. Then the people held another town-meeting, and passed resolutions justifying themselves and praising the Legislature for passing the law for which they had asked.

All this abominable outrage was perpetrated in the sober State of Connecticut, within the easy memory of the writer of this article. It reads like a romance from the Dark Ages; yet these people of Canterbury were good people, who were so much in earnest in suppressing what they believed to be a great wrong, that they were willing to be cruel toward one of the best and bravest women in their State, and to resort to mob violence, to rid themselves of an institution whose only office was to elevate the poor black children who had little chance of elevation elsewhere. Now this outrage seems just as impossible to the people of Canterbury today as it does to us. The new generation has grown clean away from it, and grown away from it so far that a school of little colored girls would, we doubt not, be welcomed there now as a praiseworthy and very interesting institution. The Connecticut girls who go South to teach in colored schools should remember or recall the time when they would not have been tolerated in their work in their own State, and be patient with the social proscription that meets them to-day. When the white man learns that a "solid South," made solid by shutting the negro from his vote, makes always a solid North, and that the solid North always means defeat, it will cease to be solid, and then the negro's vote will be wanted by two parties, and his wrong will be righted. In view of the foregoing sketch of Northern history, we can at least be charitable toward the South, and abundantly hopeful concerning the future.

11

A NATIONAL PROBLEM

Since 1865 we, the people of the United States, have been, for the most part, living "from hand to mouth," in our dealing with our national problem of the Americanized negro.

Candor requires a distinction here. Some Southern statesmen and many Northern philanthropists have really sought to lay down, broadly and deeply, the foundations of a permanent work. This is seen of all men, who can see at all, in the vast sums of money—to say nothing of personal service—that have been given for the education of the negroes in the South; also, for sustaining the Gospel among them. Most of this money, I am sure, was given "in the name of the Lord Jesus." Many of these gifts meant sacrifice to the giver. The man who would sneer at these gifts for the uplifting of ignorant negroes would have sneered with Judas when grateful and loving Mary broke her alabaster box of precious ointment and poured it upon the head of her Lord.

Most of the work that has been done is good—it will last. Some "wood, hay, and stubble" has been laid upon a good foundation. That some of the foundation-work has been laid in bad mortar and on spongy soil is not surprising to those who know that zeal does not always insure wisdom, or the purest religious experience security against mistakes of judgment. Good people, undertaking a difficult work, never had more opportunities for making mistakes. Some came with exaggerated ideas both of the degradation of the negro and of his natural capacity and disposition; others had exaggerated ideas of the depravity of Southern whites, looking at them through lenses, like the horrid things our professor showed us when we were studying "optics" long ago—distorting every face into bestial or demoniac shapes. Some, I am sorry to say, came with exaggerated ideas of their own personal excellence, and, very naturally, "fell from grace." All of them entered a work for which they were illy prepared.

I must now mention what was not creditable to either party. Few of those who came wanted advice from those who were best able to give it; and few of those who could advise were willing to give the benefit of their wisdom. Mutual suspicion, pride, and folly kept those apart who should have worked together. The secret thoughts of each might be expressed after this fashion, and, in most cases, with not much over-statement: A Northern teacher, or preacher, meets a Southern man of fairly representative character. The Northern man says in his heart: "You are a miserable traitor; a red-handed rebel; possibly you are a Ku-Klux; you hate negroes; you despise me; the 'old flag' makes you furious; you are waiting your chance to try the fight over; I will tell on you, and help to keep you down." The Southern man says in his heart: "You are a mean Yankee; a detestable carpet-bagger; a lover of negroes, (he was not over-careful of orthography or of orthoepy;) you are a 'Union Leaguer;' you are an incendiary; you mean to teach and to enforce 'social equality;' I must watch you, and keep you from putting me down and the bottom-rail on top." In most cases never were men more mistaken in each other, and partly because each had just enough truth in his notion of the other to make his misconceptions fatal. If angels ever weep and devils ever laugh, these mistaken and suspicious men furnished rich and rare occasion. Meanwhile the poor negro suffered from both sides, ground to powder by these two millstones, the upper and the nether, wearing each other out with useless friction and all-consuming heat.

In heaven's name let us now consider whether we have not had quite enough of this wretched farce which has bordered close upon a mournful tragedy!

Both sides made cruel mistakes, meantime confusing, perplexing, and frightening the negro; also spoiling him, for the noise made over him gave him an altogether overweening idea of his own importance—a state of mind highly unfavorable to his true progress in learning and in experience very needful for him.

For a time the negro was looking, with the wonder and simplicity of a child watching for Santa Claus to drop down the chimney on Christmas night, for "forty acres and a mule." Hundreds of ignorant white people expected that they, under some form of law, if not by compulsion without form, would be called on to furnish both the mule and the land. When people had been catechised by a "lieutenant with his squad" of soldiers, they did not know what to expect next. (But I protest I never expected to be called on for a mule; indeed, I had none.) And lieutenants, teachers, preachers, explorers, "developers," Freedmen's-Bureau men, Freedmen's-Aid-Society men, shrewd men "looking about," good women "looking around"—all, in the common judgment, were carpet-baggers, and all suspected. And, of a truth, some of them, "clothed in a little brief authority," did "cut fantastic tricks before high heaven," that made even wise men mad, whether the "angels wept" or not.

In a thousand ways both parties have made cruel mistakes— mistakes that sometimes issued in crimes—due in part to ignorance; in part to suspicion; in part to pride; in part to the exultations of triumph; in part to the bitterness of defeat, and always to that truth-hiding prejudice that is born of these ill-favored tempers.

The Southern people, as a class, have never since the war set themselves fairly and earnestly to the solution of this race-involving problem. Some of us have not, it seems, as yet found out that we have a problem to solve at all. We have, indeed, tried many things, some of them foolish, none of them effective. A few desperate and lawless men, to the dismay and horror of the mass of the Southern people, have sometimes tried wicked measures, as, for instance, the deviltry of Ku-Kluxism. With few exceptions our best efforts have been temporary expedients. Our work has been tentative; I might say palliative, much like the work of some

"Relief Committees" that issue rations to the hungry, but in such a blundering way as to increase pauperism.

I neither accuse nor defend; I am trying to state facts. Yet, without entering on a plea of defense, it may be asked, Whether, for at least a decade after the war, "the state of things" existing in the South made it possible for Southern people, who truly desired to know and to do right, to enter upon any broad and permanent work for the solution of our difficult problem? The plain truth is, we were struggling for existence, and though, with thousands of us, the struggle is still at its intensest point, the South has wrought wonders. No people of our times have been called on to make just such an experiment as was given to us. And we have wrought so well, notwithstanding an undeserved reputation for indolence, that no prostrated people of coming times can despair when they consider the material recuperation of our section since the utter disorganization and collapse that followed Appomattox.

No political party, as such, has dealt fairly with this question of the negro's citizenship. They have considered him almost exclusively as a voter, one party seeking to control his vote, the other seeking to avoid being controlled by it. Neither party has considered him in the fullness of his citizenship. The leaders and whippers-in have been far more anxious to count his vote than to prepare him for it.

The negro's ballot is, indeed, important in every view of the case, but in our dealings with him his importance as a voter has been greatly exaggerated by both parties, and much to his damage as a man and a citizen in the broader sense. In no rational view of the case is this a question that one political party or section of the country can solve alone. If both parties and both sections working together can solve it, they will do well. It would be a misfortune to the country if either one of the parties could solve it independently of the other party.

This is not a party or sectional problem, *it is the task of the Nation.*

It is time for all concerned, for the negroes and the whites, to know that Northern people alone, that Southern people alone cannot manage satisfactorily this question of six millions of free negroes, a full million of them voters, with millions more to come. Northern people will yet learn, what many of them do not know at this time, that this problem cannot be rightly and happily solved without the help, the cordial and vigorous co-operation, of the Southern whites. Neither of the three parties—the Northerners, the Southerners, nor the negroes—have clearly understood this absolute necessity of co-operation, though I do believe the negroes have come nearest to the truth.

It is essential, if permanent good is to be done, to understand that this national race problem requires the intelligent and hearty co-operation of three classes—Northern white people, Southern white people, and the negroes themselves. If all the Northern people were doing their best, the Southern people standing aloof in sullen silence, much might be done, but the work would be marred and hindered in all directions; so if the whole South should do its best, with the North watching with only interest enough to be censorious and critical. Neither nor both can do much if the negroes fail to do their own part.

Time does wonders; we have nearly come to the place where both sides, the North and the South, can look on this negro question in a dry light. The lava has cooled that so long rushed from both craters. At all events, there are enough men and women on both sides who can be reasonable to begin to clear the ground for mutual understanding. As to the "utter irreconcilables" on both sides, (for be it remembered that "Bourbonism" is not exclusively a Southern product,) the wiser and better people must do God's work of to-day and to-morrow without their help, and, if it come to that, in spite of their opposition. The majority hardly ever gets right on any advanced issue till after the fight is won; the minority has always led the world's progress, carrying meanwhile much dead weight.

"Stalwarts" we need, but stalwarts for country, not for party. Neither party is worth the country; possibly both put together are not absolutely essential to its salvation. The platforms upon which presidential campaigns have been conducted for twelve years past read strangely alike, considering the noise and smoke of battle that asseverated their infinite and eternal difference. Really there is not enough in the fight of parties to justify the expenditure of the whole force of a "stalwart "nature in the interests of a mere party triumph. It is a good time, surely, for earnest and yet reasonable people to agree as to what needs to be done for the whole country, and to work together to accomplish it.

The negroes, too, are in better temper to do their part. Several misconceptions as to what freedom meant they have outgrown. For one thing, they have learned, or they are fast learning, that they, as well as white men, are still under the blessed law of labor; "blessed," although they know it not. They no longer look to the government for "rations." The dream of "forty acres and a mule" has faded from their imagination.[1]

One other thing they were slow to learn, but they have nearly learned it—that neither party cares as much for them as it cares

---

[1]Just as I had written the first sentence of this paragraph a neighbor, the Rev. Nicholas Graves, a colored local preacher of the Methodist Episcopal Church, dropped into my office. As he had volunteered to bring my morning's mail before breakfast, and now appeared, though unasked, with an armful of wood, and proceeded to make so hot a fire that I could hardly stay in the room, I knew something was to be "brought forward." Nick, when freedom came, retained the surname of his old master, a wealthy planter in our county. There was much changing of names soon after emancipation, the negroes generally taking the most aristocratic name they had ever been connected with. Nick stuck to Graves, as he could not well improve upon it.

I generally give him "rope," and let him bring up his case in his own way, for his mental methods are an amusing study. But I was too busy to wait this morning. So I laid down my pen and opened the way:

"Well, Nick, what is it?"

To my amusement, he proceeded to tell me a long story about a "mule trade" he had been trying to make. He wound up by telling me that the mule trade was "off," but that "a tolable chunk of a hoss was offered him for $40." Whereupon I read him the sentence I had written, and gave him the others in the paragraph off-hand, and then looked at him. There was a display of ivory only possible to his race.

"Now, Nick, tell me, did any of them ever tell your people that?"

"Yes, sah; Mr. H., who teeched here jest after de wah, told us dat; I heered him myself."

"Nick, what did he do it for?"

"Dunno, sah, but he said it shore. He said de gubment would gib us forty acres and a mule apiece, and perwisions to last a year."

"Nick, you all voted on his side, did you?"

I did not push the subject. Cruikshanks should have seen the droll look that came into his eyes and spread over his face. But he went away happy, having received the little favor "bout de hoss trade" his soul longed for. I have often favored him; he has never "gone back" on me.

for their votes. And this lesson, when fully learned, will tone them up somewhat.

Patronage has done little for them; there are now and have ever been enough hungry camp-followers of white blood to appropriate even the "crumbs that fall from the masters table." It is hard to keep up their interest in politics, seeing that neither party, North nor South, has office for them. Even the Indian lost interest in the hunt when his white partner always took the "turkey" and left him the "buzzard." But, badinage aside, it is a fact most important and encouraging to all who wish the negro well, that the comparative subsidence of his fierce political fever promises the best results for his true progress in all good things. The negro can now co-operate with his friendly helpers, whether of the North or of the South, as he could not have done even four years ago.

One other thought as to this race problem, I wish to stress at this point. While its right solution is vastly important to every part of the Republic, it is absolutely vital to us of the South. Its right solution concerns the Southern white man only less than it concerns the negro himself. Possibly I ought not to say "only less," for the fortunes of these two races in the South are inextricably mixed. They cannot get away from each other. What might have been if history had been different; what we would choose if things were not as they are—these speculations are idle. Instead of dreaming about the civilization we would build up with materials that we have not, it is the part of men of sense to do the best they can with what they have in hand. If we of the South cannot get on with the negro; if the negro cannot get on with us; then we two peoples cannot get on at all. For we are here, both of us, and here to stay. But get on we must, somehow and at some speed. Much we have done; more we can and will do. When we consider how Providence has blessed our efforts we see ten thousand reasons for hopefulness. Croaking is ingratitude, and it is treason. If our progress, however slow, is only in the right direction, all will be well by and by. If we cannot go fast, we must go slow, but we must go.[2]

---

[2] The late venerable and eloquent Dr. Lovick Pierce, who never missed a chance, during a ministry of seventy-five years, to do the negroes good, was preaching once on Christian

We white people of the South have more at stake in this race-problem than other white men and women of any nation can have. And it is now full time that we should do our best thinking, working, and praying over this problem of a free negro race in our midst—a race that has been, is now, and forever will be, an integral part of our industrial, social, and political system. If, for any reasons whatsoever, we of the South refuse to do, or fail to do, our part of this work, there will be loss all round—loss that can never be compressed into or expressed by statistical tables. The Southern whites lose, the negro loses, the world loses. But I am deeply impressed that there is a difference. The world can get on without the South much better than the South can get on without the world. This may not be a brilliant discovery; but a goodly number have not yet made it.

But there is a lesson the Northern people have never fully mastered; and it is very important to all parties that they should learn it. If the best results are to follow the efforts many Northern people are making to elevate the negro, they must realize, as they never have done, the absolute necessity of Southern co-operation. Would God this might be learned by all sides to this question before it is too late! Millions of money poured forth, and thousands of precious lives exhausted upon, this problem, will not avail for its full and right solution without Southern co-operation. Many of the North have had glimpses of this truth, but they seem not to understand it fully; else, surely they would have tried harder and more wisely to secure the help they need, and that we only can give. Many in the South have had glimpses also; but few of us, if any, have had the clear vision of our duty and our opportunity; else, surely, we would have been more ready to help in every "good

---

Progress at a camp-meeting. It was his manner to make astonishing climaxes now and then. On this occasion he laid down the law of life and death in Christian experience: "Brethren, you must grow or die. Progress you must make. If you can fly, fly; if you can't fly, run; if you can't run, walk; if you can't walk, crawl." His voice was rising to its full trumpet tones, and his eye flashing as few eyes ever flashed. His right hand was still high advanced. The congregation trembled for him. What could he say more? But he was the master of such a crisis. He wound up the sentence with an explosion like thunder: "If you can't crawl—*worm it along!*"

word and work." Heaven pardon our blindness! but there has been so much smoke of powder and other things that we could not always see our way.

Can any thing in the world be plainer? A candy shop cannot succeed in a hostile community. Much less can a school or a Church.

What must become of all the noble schemes of Northern benevolence in the negroes' behalf, if the stronger and more numerous race, in the very midst of which he lives, and moves, and has his being, whose tenant he is, whose influence he can no more escape than he can escape the atmosphere he breathes, if this race is either hostile or indifferent to the efforts that are being made to do him good and to lift him up? Much the Northern people have done with little help from us; much they can and will do without our help; but they can and will do unspeakably more with it. What waste of energy, what spoiling of noble schemes of usefulness, what hinderance to our own progress as well as the negroes', what marring of what ought to be a divinely beautiful and beneficent work, must result from foolish and sinful antagonism in feeling and purpose and method between the white man from the North and the white man in the South!

I do not believe that there is any thing insuperable between these two men. They are not fools, though they exhibit folly upon occasion; they are not visionary, though they are sometimes impracticable; they are not relentless, though they are sometimes hot of temper; they are not blind, though they are sometimes slow to learn; they will yet be fraternal, though they have been hard and stubborn fighters through many years and on many fields. These men will yet understand one another. Perhaps not to-morrow. Well, then, after a while, when the blindest of us, on either side, are silent in death.

Let us think on this! Ten years toward the close of a generation's life makes a great difference. Wise men, in Church as well as State, who have read history, and who know human nature, both in its strength and weakness, will take the fact and law of mortality—most beneficent law it is!—into their estimates for future times and relations.

Nothing is more certain than this, and yet many leaders, who ought to know and do not "know what Israel ought to do," are forgetful or blind. An impulse of passion or sentiment that carries the policy that prevails through one generation cannot be depended on for the next. If we trust a great policy to such a current, it is as if one should undertake to navigate a little river swollen with a summer flood: such a stream cannot be depended on—it runs out. The great ship had better trust the sea—so wide and deep. And if we have any great policy for Churches or States, nothing is deep enough to float us above all rocks and shoals but principles that are eternally right.

The impulses that broke out in war in 1861, having given forth many premonitory mutterings before that time, are already exhausting themselves. The grave is, next to grace, the greatest extinguisher of wrath. Before now the "white rose" of York and the "red rose" of Lancaster have blended their colors. A great passion in Church or Nation runs its course, like a fever; the patient recovers and the fever dies; or fever and patient die together. The great tidal wave of 1854, that overwhelmed the town of Samoda in Japan, had sunk to a few inches when it broke against the firm coast of California. The slight recoil was never felt in the far China Sea. We sometimes forget how wide and deep is the ocean of human life.

If the spirit of wisdom and grace be in them, these white men of the North and these white men of the South will yet understand each other, they will yet bury their antagonisms in spite of differences that may be beyond their control—differences good "after their kind"; and each working out, as God enables him, his own duty and destiny, they will at last unite to perform a common duty to their dark-skinned brother, brought so strangely to our country and delivered to our care that the great and worldwide plans of the Father of all for the good of all may be fairly and fully accomplished.

12

THE METHODS OF OUR PROBLEM

One thing I assume as settled forever: such a problem as we have in hand never was solved, never can be solved, on any theory or system of mere repression. There has been no lack of experiments. History teems with examples, both in ancient and in modern times. As well try to prevent volcanic eruptions by shutting down our little furnace gates upon the fires that burn at the heart of the earth.

Repression may well be called the Egyptian theory of government; Pharaoh made long trial of it, with what result the world knows. It is the Russian theory now; it has failed notably, and men wait to see what explosions and disasters are yet to come. Repression has failed in Ireland. It has not succeeded with our American Indians. It was tried for generations on Hungary and failed utterly. The method of recognition, of lifting up, has been tried in Hungary only a few years and it succeeds. This method always succeeds; the other always fails. The system of mere repression fails everywhere, in the family, the school, the factory, the State, the Church. Rome has made every possible use of repression. If it succeeded after a fashion, during the Dark Ages, it fails now that all men, as well as Galileo, have found "that the world does move." The repressive system is tyranny. It violates the divine will; it is out of harmony with eternal righteousness; it subverts the order of nature as well as of grace. Mere repression cannot succeed where there is life, except to destroy. But it is not always that it destroys the proposed victim; it destroyed Pharaoh; Israel was delivered out of his hands. There are other such instances, and very instructive they are.

The problem before us, the Northern and Southern people together, and the Southern people in particular, is the right education and elevation of our black brother, the free negro, in our midst. Do not, beloved white brother, scare at this word "elevation." Nothing is said about putting the "negro above the white man." Let me whisper a secret in your ear: *That cannot be done unless you get below him.* Think of this, and if you find yourself underneath blame yourself. The negro cannot rise simply because he is black; the white man cannot stay up simply because he is white. A man rises, not by the color of his skin, but by intelligence, industry, and integrity. The foremost man in these excellences and virtues must, in the long run, be also the highest man. And it ought to be so. Ignorance, indolence, immorality, have no right to rise. Let the white man rise as high as he can, providing always that he does not rise by wrongs done to another. In such rising there is no real elevation. And let every other man rise to his full stature, the white, the black, the red, the yellow. No honest man, with brains in his head, doubts for one moment that it is God's will that every man he ever made of every race, should make the most of his "talents" his Creator gave him. Therefore are talents given, that every man may be just as much of a man as he can be. The King at his coming will demand his own "with usury." There is no more sacred right, than a man's right to be all that God gives him ability to be in all good things. The divine Magna Charta guarantees this right. There is no higher duty than that each human being do his utmost to realize the fullest possibilities of his life. Whatever hinders does infinite damage to all concerned.

These chapters are not written for philosophers, statesmen, scholars, or for any who imagine themselves filled with all knowledge, but for my neighbors and fellow-citizens who, like the writer, realize somewhat the difficulty as well as the magnitude of this race problem that Providence has given us to work out. No exhaustive discussions are proposed in these pages; indeed, the fullest statement could not say all that belongs to this many-sided and far-reaching subject.

If the question be asked, How may we get our dark brother prepared for his duty of citizenship? I prefer to change the form of the question. Let us rather ask, How can we help our brother prepare himself for his calling and duty of citizenship? Growth is from within; no amount of work done upon the negro can make him what he ought to be and can be. He must grow into his right manhood and citizenship. The white race has reached its higher estate by processes of growth. We started low down and it has taken a long time. We are not half grown yet. We also may meditate profitably on Isaiah li, I.

Doing things for, and giving things, to people does not lift them up, if the doing and the giving do not spring a new hope, a new aspiration, a new purpose in them, or, in some way, vivify into fruitful life some dormant good already in their souls. The test of our usefulness to others is to be found in their character. Do we make them wiser, stronger, braver, truer? Then we have lifted them up by helping them to grow out of their weakness and evil into their strength and goodness. Why is it better to give a poor man a day's work than a day's rations without the work? The one gift lifts him up, the other pauperizes him. In all our plans and efforts to lift up the negro let us remember that our best help to him is whatever most effectually enables him to help himself.

We are asking, many of us in the North and in the South, what can we do? I know not that I can help any to the answer for them. I will be grateful if I can answer for myself. This much is clear to me: common sense and common justice must be our guide. Fine-spun theories are too gossimer for the tough work before us. Pretty sentiments may grace drawing-rooms, and win applause at "anniversaries," but our work is to be done in smoky cabins, in our own kitchens, in cotton and corn fields, in shops, in little school-houses, in humble chapels, in court-rooms, in a word, in whatever places this poor and untaught brother's currents of life and labor carry him. I have said nothing of legislative halls and methods, because it seems clear that neither acts of Congress nor of State Legislatures can reach all the obscure corners of our daily and hourly relations to each other.

By every token, the laws must provide for his citizenship, just as they provide for the white man's, no more, no less. But let us not make the fatal mistake of supposing that the mere enactment of good laws will meet the myriad complications and difficulties of this subject.

No perfect scheme, with finished statement of details, can be drawn out in advance. The experiment will, as it proceeds, indicate new needs, while the effort will develop new resources and methods for meeting them. Undoubtedly, the first and main thing is to have *the right spirit.* If all parties concerned really wish to succeed, and thoroughly purpose to do their best, success is sure. A thorough-going, honest purpose to do our best will wonderfully sharpen our wits as to the best methods, and as wonderfully multiply our resources for working them successfully. There is no man so dull in inventing ways and means as the man who feels no interest or conscience in his duties, and whose chief pleasure is in avoiding them.

This new citizen is a voter, and, unhappily for all, he is not ready for his responsibilities. Voting means choosing, and wise choosing means intelligence. Woe to the land where those who hold the balance of power are in ignorance. This tremendous engine of political power, the ballot, must be in hands that know what they are doing. This voter *must be educated.* Nothing can be plainer than this. He who, in 1881, needs to have this proved to him is incapable of reasoning.

I will not entangle my argument with the question of the relative capacity of the white and black races, nor will I speculate about the African's capacity for "high culture." My argument has nothing to do with these questions; let the schools and colleges make out of him the utmost that it is in him to make. Then let the world measure him by what he does. If any fear that he will, when at his fullest growth, be too great a man, let *them* grow, or organize an "exodus," and find a place where they will be free from his overshadowing greatness. My argument concerns his education in the three "Rs." If any thing in this world is settled, it is settled that the negro can learn to read, to write, and to "cipher." And he learns well and rapidly. I want no proof beyond what I have seen with my own eyes and heard with my own ears. He can learn a great deal more, but these parts of knowledge he must learn for his safety and ours. These are the keys; give them to him, and let him unlock all the doors of wisdom he can. This is fair; it is wise; it is necessary; it is right.

This new power in our social and political system must be educated, and for the same reason that white illiteracy must be educated. The negro's case is the more exigent only because there is a larger percentage of ignorance in his race. An ignorant voter, of whatever color he may be, is a constant menace and a certain injury to the purity of elections. As a voter, therefore, the negro must be taught. But we must go beyond the mere voter. His wife, his daughter, must be educated also, else the race will not be educated; the need is to *teach the race*.

How can this race be educated? And how can the work be done most promptly and wisely? I claim no mastery of this question, for it is very large and very complicated. Perhaps no one man will claim to see all its sides, to see through it and to master it altogether. This I know, some have failed because they thought they had mastered it. Some things that seem clear to me I venture to suggest, feeling my way to the wisdom and truth of the matter with such light as I have, and holding myself ready to follow any who have more light to guide our steps.

1. The first thing of all to do is the simplest, yet, perhaps, the most difficult—*clear the way*. Remove all hinderances; make the paths straight—not strait; give him the best chance possible to him. If all this were done the problem would, by and by, solve itself. To do this, to give him this best chance possible to him, it is not impossible that some of us white people of the South must, first of all, put ourselves through a course of schooling in right views on this subject. If we have prejudices that prevent us from thoroughly investigating this matter, as if there were contamination in

the very subject itself, let us make haste to purify ourselves from such prejudices. For such prejudices there is need of the "hyssop branch." People who give money and send their sons and daughters to convert the heathen over the seas should be ashamed of such nonsense. It is to be hoped that few among us indulge such weaknesses; it is to be prayed that there will soon be none among us in so great darkness of mind and badness of heart.

But let us avoid mere sentimentalism; we are dealing with very practical things. No amount of correct thinking and of good feeling can meet all the demands of this case. There are some things the white people cannot do for the negro; it would be a misfortune if they could. For example, they cannot give him leisure for his schooling and his studies; in some way he must create this for himself. This race cannot throw down its hoe and take up its spelling-book at the movement of a wand. These people must work, ought to work, for their living. There is no help for it, and there ought to be no help for it. This necessity is not based upon their poverty only, nor at all in the color of their skin, but in their physical, mental, moral, and social constitution as human beings. It is the primal law for all men of every color and condition. An unworking race cannot be truly educated, for labor is itself a part of education. If some power could feed and clothe and shelter them by the distribution of all things needful for their bodies, could dismiss them from their toils and send the whole race to school for a term of years, the problem of the negro's right education would not be solved, although every one mastered a liberal course of studies. Such schooling would create new and harder problems; under such conditions their moral and social education could not keep pace with their mental development, and thus a new and deadly virus would be introduced into their very blood. One obvious result would be, such education would multiply vagabonds and sharpers by the million. For true education means far more than "book learning"; there must be education of the instincts, the feelings, the habits, the will, the conscience. But, assuredly, whatever hinderances to his education there may be that are not rooted in the very necessity and nature of things should be put out of his way. He should have every chance he can well employ. He has no right to ask more; we have no right to give less. There should be no opposition, active or passive. It is to be hoped that there is now little opposition to his education; there should be none.

2. He should be encouraged and cheered to do his utmost. Right motives should be brought to bear upon him. He should be taught how dangerous to himself, how hurtful to all, is citizenship with ignorance. He should be taught, as white people who do not know should be taught, that ignorance is always weakness, and that voluntary ignorance is a shame and a sin. He should be taught that he who can secure instruction for his children, and will not, sins against his children, his country, and his God. He should be taught to feel himself branded with infamy when he can and will not save his children from the curse and bondage of ignorance. He should be taught that slavery lurks in ignorance; it may not be slavery to a recognized and responsible master, but, worst of all, slavery to the powers of darkness. (Alas! there are thousands of white people among us—let any deny who will—who need to learn these first lessons of true fatherhood and motherhood.) He should be brought to see the value and blessedness of knowledge—not merely the learning of books and of the schools, but of all knowledge that can help to make him wise and good as a man. The negro is more ready to receive this lesson than many suppose. For him, and for all like him, is the promise of that word of Christ, "Blessed are they which do hunger and thirst, ... for they shall be filled."

3. He should be encouraged to do his utmost to help himself—to be a self-supporting man. To make the negro's education, or any other man's, an absolute gratuity is a grievous mistake. The philosophy of this principle goes deeper than the skin. It is rooted in the very constitution of human nature. One of the most important parts of education is, learning, so that they enter into every fiber of the character, the sentiments and habits of manly and womanly personal independence. How different the case of two

fathers, indeed of two families, where in one case the education of a son or daughter costs them nothing; where in the other case they have, at least, done what they could! For example: During our last vacation, in the summer of 1880, a Georgia farmer talked with me one day about sending his son to college. This is what he said: "We have one child, this son; we are poor, but when he was a little boy we determined to send him some day. My wife and I found that, by close economy, we could lay up about $100 each year; we have now $600 in bank for his education. Two years ago, as soon as he was old enough, I gave him a cotton patch that he might make enough himself to meet his incidental expenses. The first year he made $25; the second, $50; this year he may make something more than $50."

How wise is this father, this mother, this son! Such a plan worked out is itself an education. If his education go no further, would the best college training that cost no forethought, economy, loving self-denial, be worth as much in making a man of this boy?

Of course this question of the negro's education concerns, almost exclusively, the children and youth of the race. If the education of these children should be made absolutely a free-gift, three evils, each of them grave, would follow: 1. The negro father would not depend on himself as the head of his family; 2. The process must be kept up indefinitely; 3. Many of the negro's weakest traits of character will be perpetuated. But if the present generation of negroes are encouraged to help themselves somewhat in educating their children—it may be but little, but it should be enough for them to "feel it"—if they are taught how they may help themselves, the next generation will take up the task more vigorously and more intelligently. Thus, and thus only, will the habit of helping themselves become the habit of the race. How sorely this habit is now needed in them only they can understand who know, from experience, how completely the system of slavery provided for all their wants that, under that system, were expected to be met. The slave had nothing to do but work; every thing—shelter, clothes, food, medicine, and support in old age—was provided for him.

He could not acquire any habit of forethought or instinct of saving. He never felt the necessity; he never saw the occasion.[1]

4. But the negroes must have help from without for a generation at least. Their poverty makes this a necessity, as poverty—utter poverty—makes help necessary for not a few white people. When I say help, I mean *help*, not the transfer of the entire burden to other shoulders.

It is not simply their need, but it is the economy of all to help them. To put the argument on its lowest plane, it is cheaper to teach them than it is to meet the increased expenses of government that grow inevitably out of ignorance. Surely this statement needs neither argument nor illustration. It is very penny-wise and pound-foolish to withhold the help needful to enable them to help themselves to an education. There is no escape for avarice, twist and turn as it may; if it will not build school-houses and churches it must build jails. Thus reason and justice get their grim revenge.

Where is the money to come from to help them?

1. Partly from the "public-school" systems of the States, counties, and municipalities. Most of our Southern State systems are appallingly inadequate. The States do not support their school systems except in a meager manner. I believe the School Com-

---

[1]A few mechanics among them managed to save handsome sums of money. Sometimes such a man "hired his own time," the master giving him a good "margin." The following incident will illustrate the exceptional cases, and show how singular were some of their views. The father-in-law of one of the professors in Emory College was a Virginian of property. He owned a quick-witted shoemaker rated at $2,500. The master allowed Edmund—that was his name—to "hire himself" at such figures that, in the course of some years, he accumulated between two and three thousand dollars. His master loved him, and offered to sell him to himself for $1,200—a little less than half price. Edmund took the matter into serious consideration, and declined the offer with this statement of the case: "See here, Mars Mack, I can't 'ford to own any $1,200 nigger; s'pose I lay down and die, I lose dis money." It turned out well for Edmund. He got his freedom "without money and without price," and saved his own cash. He loaned enough to "Mars Mack" to start his business again. As to himself, he did not "stick to his last." He went into politics, was elected to the Virginia Constitutional Convention, and became a "leader" of more than average sense. Poor fellow! he was killed, with so many others, in the crush-in of the Capitol in Richmond.

missioners have done all that could be done with the pitiful sums of money at their command.

2. Partly from the Nation, as many wise men urge. (I am not sure of this.)

3. The people of the North should put a great deal of money in this work. Little more than the South itself can the North afford to bear the burden and peril to free institutions that come through millions of untaught negro citizens. Many of these good people have given to this work with princely liberality. But they should give more, and continue to give. There are at least two reasons that they will recognize: 1) They made the negro a voter before he was ready, and now, by every token, they should do their best to get him ready as soon as possible. 2. They have the money. I am glad they have wealth, for many of them make good use of it. I know of no people in the world who give so much money to the cause of education. It is an immortal honor to them. Recognizing their good deeds and great gifts in the past, I say, nevertheless, they should give more abundantly. For they have, by God's blessing the money. The work to be done is very great, and it cannot wait without grievous loss. Moreover, the North has already invested too much money in this problem to stop now; *they cannot afford to stop.*

4. The Southern people should give money to help educate the negro. I do not mean only give it as States, in the payment of taxes; but as individuals, they should, when they are able—and some are able—give money to this cause. If they would help more, perhaps they would be richer.[2]

He was a close observer and a wise thinker who said: "There is that scattereth, and yet increaseth; and there is that withholdeth more than is meet, but it tendeth to poverty."

---

[2]After this chapter was written I was informed that a citizen of Georgia, an ex-Confederate and ex-slave-holder of high degree, had subscribed or given $5,000 to build a college for colored people, under the patronage of one of the colored Churches in a city in Georgia. His promise is a bond, his paper "gilt-edge" at any bank. All honor to him; may many imitate his example!

The details of these ways and means are not to be argued here. But "if there be first a willing mind," ways and means will be found.

13

Schools for Negroes

There should be separate schools for negro children. It is best for all parties. However it may be in other sections or countries, it is not best to mix the races in Southern school-rooms. Right or wrong, wise or foolish, this is a fact. All but lunatics and visionaries recognize facts. From our stand-point the Chinaman is silly for sticking to his cue—the memorial and badge of his subjection to an alien race—with such invincible obstinacy. But the cue is dear to his "celestial" soul, and the wise missionary does not destroy his chance to do him good by stressing an unnecessary issue about hair. Wise reformers will consider even the weaknesses of the people they would lift up, just as wise doctors consider the peculiarities of their patients. I have known a lady thrown into hysterics by the presence of cats. What sort of doctor would he be who would prescribe cats for her hysteria—cats tied to her bedstead? If a doctor discovers that the smell of garlic produces nausea in a nervous patient, will he insist that the only chance for a cure is in mixing garlic juice in every drop of water the patient drinks? Not unless he is a quack of the first water.

Now "the facts" are these: 1. Southern white children, as a class, won't sit at the same desks with negro children; 2. Southern black children, as a class, don't want to sit at the same desks with white children. And this gives trouble to no soul of man, except to a small class of fanatics, who feel that all things human must yield to their fancies.

Let us grant, if any desire it, that these white children have not been delivered from the spirit of caste, and that these black children do not assert their rights. Neither the pride of the one nor the weakness of the other can be denied as facts—as facts that must be considered. But as things are, and as they are likely to continue to be till we are all dead who are troubled about such things, or until it please God to create new and different races of people, this mutual desire and willingness for separation are right. For this race-separation should not cease at the expense of the white child's sincerity or of the black child's self-respect. Sincerity and self-respect are more important than sitting together, even granting the advantages that have been claimed for the plan. Practically, Northern and Southern people are much alike in their feelings on such subjects; if they had had our history perhaps they would, on this too-much-talked-of matter, be neither better nor worse than we are.[1]

The colored schools should have the support, countenance, (there is much in this word countenance,) indorsement, and co-operation of Southern white people. Reasonable and good people

---

[1] In Cincinnati, Ohio, May, 1880, a very "stalwart" gentleman pressed me closely on what he called the wrong of our Southern caste feelings. Said I:

"Have you none of this feeling?"

"None," he answered promptly, looking me straight in the eye. "With us the color of the skin has nothing to do with social recognition. It is simply a question of personal culture."

It occurred to me at once that he had not been tested by experiment, the color-culture not, perhaps, reaching the proper standard; for I had met, in their great hotels and at some of their best homes, no colored people except as waiters; but I had found the man I had long been looking for, so I ventured one more question:

"Tell me now, candidly, upon your conscience, if, seeking a place to sleep, you were to be ushered into a room with two double beds in it, with a clean white man in one bed and a clean negro in the other, and you had free choice, which bed would you get in?"

He looked so straight at me that I thought he was going to say, "In with the negro." But I was mistaken; poor human nature put his philosophy to flight. After a moment's silence, looking upon the floor this time; he answered slowly and sadly:

"I would get in with the white man."

On that answer we "fraternized." Now, if my Cincinnati friend had been a negro, and equally candid, he would have said: "I would get in with the black man." The true doctrine I suppose is about this: "Let every man be fully persuaded in his own mind." This is not contrary to the "Civil Rights' Bill." That bill does not give to any color the right to require any other color to sleep with it, or sit by it. It only, in this respect, grants the privilege where both are agreed.

must feel kindly toward schools for negroes; if they do not, they are ignorant. To do its best work in a community a colored school needs more than money-help and the mere toleration that allows it to exist—it needs moral and social support. How this is to be afforded must be determined by sensible people on the merits of each case.

Some things I may mention as illustrations of many methods of encouragement and help. The school may be visited by proper persons at reasonable hours. The pastor of the white Church close by could do good in this way. Some of them do; all of us might and ought. Official people might encourage the school by an occasional visit, as the mayor, the village squire, the teacher of the white school, and other persons of influence and local consideration. The teacher should be treated kindly and respectfully, and made to understand that he has the favor and support of all good people. Any outrage by "lewd fellows of the baser sort" should be taken in hand and punished promptly, certainly, and with such severity as the law provides and the case demands.

If, on other grounds, the teacher is entitled to personal and social recognition, the fact of his teaching a negro school should be no bar. Think, for example, of people admiring David Livingstone, and then turning up their noses at a teacher, not because he is bad, or ignorant, or ill-bred, nor yet even because he is a negro, but, forsooth, because he teaches a negro school! There is a very large intimation of "sham" in this distinction without a difference.

If the work of educating the negroes of the South is ever to be carried on satisfactorily, if ever the best results are to be accomplished, then *Southern white people must take part in the work of teaching negro schools.*

There have been some very sad and hurtful mistakes in the relations assumed by most of us of the South to this whole matter, and especially in the fact that, with very rare exceptions, our people have steadfastly refused to teach negro children, especially since they were made free, for love or money. They have recoiled from negro schools as if there were personal degradation in teaching them. Perhaps the state of things that existed at the South for a full decade after the war, and for which Southern people were not alone responsible—a state of things that made it impracticable for Southern white men and women to teach negro schools—was inevitable. But so it was; they could not do it without "losing caste." As I am trying to state facts honestly I should add, the prevailing sentiment of the South would not even now look favorably upon such teachers. (But I must say we are growing in sense as well as grace on this subject.) And this sentiment would feel more kindly toward a Northern man or woman teaching a negro school than toward a Southerner. It is much easier to denounce the sentiments that underlie this state of things than to cure them. Let our Northern friends, who are now happily free, as they tell us, from such follies, consider Canterbury Green in 1831 and 1834. They were not always so wise and good as they are now; moreover, many of them are not yet "perfect" in this grace; all have not yet "attained" this height.

But, in all truth and common sense, there is no reason for discounting, in any respect, a white man or woman simply for teaching negroes. It is utterly absurd. May it not, also, be sinful? Let us consider our attitude for a moment. We have the negroes to cook for us, and if they do not know how, as is often the case, our wives and daughters teach them. We employ them in all sorts of ways. When elections come on we ask not only their votes but *their* "social influence." Candidates, from governor to coroner, do this, earnestly, invariably, and without social discredit. We sell goods to them, we buy from them, we practice law for them, we practice medicine for them, and it is all right enough. In all business relations, except teaching, so far as I can remember our ways on this subject, whether as employers or as employés, we think it is all fair, and so do our wise neighbors. How utterly and childishly absurd it is to "make an exception" if one teaches a negro child how to spell, to read, and to write! Will some master in such fine knowledge explain just wherein it is a nice thing to sell goods to a negro or to buy from him, to practice law for him, to give him medicine, but not quite respectable to teach him whatever he can learn that we can teach?

Some have made a considerable ado about "Yankee school teachers" in the negro schools in the South, and in some cases our heathen have acted much as the heathen of Canterbury Green acted in 1831. Perhaps some of them have not been altogether to our taste; perhaps some of them have mixed in with the "three Rs" some things not to edification. But what else could be done? Would qualified Southern men and women have taken these places when the Northern teachers came? Would they do it now? Not generally, though some of the best would, as a very few of the best have begun to do. Suppose these Northern teachers had not come, that nobody had taught the negroes, set free, and citizens! The South would have been uninhabitable by this time. Some may resent this; be it so, they resent the truth.

It was St. Paul who asked the fiery and inconstant Galatians, "Am I therefore become your enemy because I tell you the truth?"

I have had good reason to believe that many of these schools would have been filled, by preference, with Southern teachers had they been available. I have reason to know, at this writing, that some good negro schools can be obtained for Southern teachers, and that they are preferred, if suitable persons can be found.

If, from this showing, our Northern friends conclude that "it is better to let these unreasonable people go, and furnish all these schools ourselves," then I tell them they will conclude hastily and unwisely. For it is most important that Southern white men and women take part in the work of teaching the negroes. And some day, assuredly, we will outgrow our childish weaknesses on this subject. May it be soon! No whim can hold its own against common sense, common interest, and religious principle.

Leaving the higher ground of duty, I affirm that every consideration of sound policy should lead Southern whites to teach negro schools. I am sure that, other things being equal, Southern teachers can do more for the advancement of negro students. Here I am driven to theory, for the most part. There has been too little experiment to put the argument on a basis of ascertained and indisputable facts. But I am reasonably confident of the soundness of the view presented. It ought to be true; for the

Southern whites understand the negroes better than other white people do or can.

Now, if it is certain that these two races, so strangely associated in the providence of God, will remain together; if it is desirable that they sustain friendly relations in the future; if it is important that they sustain mutually useful relations for all time to come, then, I conclude, although with little experiment and few facts, that Southern men and women have a great opportunity, if they will only be as wise as they are really well-disposed, and teach the children of the negroes whenever and wherever they can.

If the best man or woman in the South, if the most nobly-connected member of the "oldest and best family," should go into the wilds of Africa, as missionary, to teach Mteza's people, there is not a human creature, with sense or soul, who would not honor the mission. Who can taboo this man or woman for teaching negro children in a Georgia village, and give a rational reason for the difference? Does one say, It is the glamour of romance, the heroism, the lofty devotion, of the missionary that commands homage? This is not the whole case. If this person, instead of going to Africa to teach Mteza's children, should stay in Georgia and teach white children, there would be no social taboo. We must learn better than this; there is neither sense nor religion in discounting people, otherwise worthy, for teaching negroes. This feeling wont bear the light.

A large part of this work of educating the black race must be done by negroes themselves. It would be, in many respects, better for them if they could furnish thoroughly-trained and competent teachers for all their schools. Thanks to large-hearted and far-seeing charity north of us, and to the political sagacity of some of our Southern States, many negroes have already received education enough to make them very useful to their own people. In my own village of Oxford, one of these better-taught negroes, a young woman from one of the Atlanta training-schools, has been teaching for several months before the Christmas just passed. And this very morning, a "committee" of colored men met in my kitchen to "settle with the teacher." They had pledged themselves to "add enough" to the State "School Fund" to "make up" a salary of $26 a month. Part of this supplemental fund was made up by the parents of the colored children; part of it by contributions from colored men without children. My cook, an old bachelor, a man of fine sense and character, "put in his part." And herein Bristow Maxwell is an "ensample" unto many bachelors of lighter hue.

Very often and in many ways these colored teachers of colored schools can be greatly helped by the kind and hearty recognition of persons of influence in a community. Negroes set great store by the opinion of the village squire, doctor, or other notables. If their teachers are respected by the white leaders it increases tenfold their own respect for them, and, therefore, their power to do good. As to how such helpful recognition shall be given no rules will answer. Good sense, a kind heart, and a just spirit, will make it easy in every case. It is needless to talk of what we could or could not have done fifteen years ago. It is better to do our duty to-day than to defend the past or to be "consistent" with its mistakes. It is enough to know that we, of to-day, can now help this good work in a hundred ways. Will we do it? Most certainly—provided we be wise and have the spirit of Christ within us.

No doubt this question will take on new phases in the not distant future. It is certain that as colored men and women increase in numbers they will be in demand, by their people at least, for various services. After a while there will be many negro lawyers and doctors. And there seems to me to be no sensible reason why there should not be trained men to serve their race in these important and necessary callings. There is already in Nashville, Tennessee—city of universities—a good medical school for negroes. There is another in North Carolina, and possibly others. The opening of the "Meharry Medical College," in the spring of 1880, was attended, and the enterprise sanctioned, by many of the first men of the state and city.[2]

In all these directions of educated African talent and energy the "supply" will be regulated by the "demand." Whatever new

---

[2] One of its chief founders, Mr. Hugh Meharry, died near the close of 1880, at his home in Dement, Illinois, in a good old age, full of faith and good works.

factors in this equation the future develops, let the men of the future adjust. In these respects, at least, let the future take care of itself.

As for our part, let us observe the wise counsel of Thomas Carlyle, "Do the duty that lies nearest thee; the next will already have become plainer." We may be sure that we can, in no way, get ready for the future, if we fail to take care of the present. With or without us the future comes, with all its possibilities; and this good and necessary work of teaching and lifting up the negro race in the South will go on, with or without our help. We may greatly retard—we cannot, were we foolish enough to try, effectually or permanently hinder—its progress. But this we can do: by neglect and failure in our duty now, we can rob ourselves of vast benefits the future will bring to us, if we are faithful to-day.

There has never been a time when the negro, whether slave or freedman, has not been upon the heart and conscience of thousands of good people in the South—as good people as live in this world. Multitudes of them have tried, in many ways, to be useful to the negro. They have done unspeakably more than they have had credit for. They have not had as many opportunities, since 1865, to be useful to the negro as uninformed persons have supposed. For a long time the negro wanted little that we could give him, except wages for his work, and help when he got into trouble. Then he knew where to go. The negro himself was, for a time, exclusive; he did not care to have Southern white men in his churches or about his schools. They were taught, by evil persons, to suspect us all. But all this—explain it as any please—is changing. We are now welcomed to their pulpits as we have not been welcomed in fifteen years. On this point, I speak that I do know, and testify that I have seen.

I wish to be truthful. Many of our people have not been as prompt to accept these friendly overtures as, it seems to me, they ought to have been. Many could have done more than they have done. I think I know my neighbors and the people of the South, and I give it as my opinion that there is among us a wide-spread feeling of awakened conscience as to our relations to the negroes;

thousands of us feel, and feel deeply, that we ought to do more; and thousands of us intend to do more for their social, mental, and religious welfare. We had better excuses ten, even five, years ago than we have now. Indeed, there is little excuse for us at this time, 1881, if we fail to do a great and gracious work for the moral uplifting of the negroes. It seems to me far less important that any great scheme of things be devised than that each Christian man and woman do whatever useful thing for the negro there may come to hand. In this way the saving leaven will be diffused "till the whole be leavened." For example, it came to my knowledge some time ago that a little boy, in his eleventh year, has been for some time teaching a negro man thirty years old, and a servant in his father's family, to read and "add sums." Why cannot this little effort be repeated in half a million Southern families at once, and without the intervention of a "society" or the appropriation of a dollar? What a harvest would follow! what new inspirations! what re-awakening of kindly affections! what cementing of friendly ties! what light and truth and grace, with God's blessings on both races and upon the whole country!

14

SOME WORK GOOD PEOPLE ARE DOING

No honest man who can read and understand statistics will study the United States Census, or the Annual Reports of the Honorable Commissioner of Education, and deny that there is an appalling mass of illiteracy in the Southern States, both among the white people and the negroes. As to the illiteracy of the negroes, (who make the vast majority of untaught people in the South) something may be said in extenuation. As to illiteracy among the white people of the South, I do not know any excuse good enough to offer. *I wish I did.*

In the United States Senate, December 15, 1880, the Hon. Joseph E. Brown, one of the senators from Georgia, delivered an able speech on the "Bill to Establish an Educational Fund," etc. A few paragraphs I quote because they state fairly a case not fully understood, it seems. Senator Brown, after describing the processes by which the negro became a freeman and a voter, proceeds to state the attitude of the South toward the question of his education then and now. The senator said:

> A grave problem arises here for solution. They must be educated; but we are not able to educate them. Why not? We claimed to be a wealthy people before the war. So we were; but we lost, according to the best estimates, about two billions of dollars in the value of our slaves. It was that much gold value, our own under the Constitution of the United States, which we lost by the war, and it was gone forever. That impoverished us to that extent, and it was a very heavy draft. Then we had to support the Confed-

erate armies for four years, without a dollar of help, out of our substance. True, we issued Confederate bonds and notes; they were paid out of our substance, but at the end of the war they were repudiated, and they became as ashes in our hands. We lost, then, not only two billions in slaves, but we lost about two billions more in the support of our armies for four years. Then we lost immense amounts in the destruction of property by the armies outside of what was necessary to feed and clothe them.

But that was not all. At the end of the struggle we had to return to the Union and resume our position, and take upon ourselves our just proportion, according to our means, of the war debt contracted by the government in the suppression of what is known as the Rebellion. Then, I say, with these drafts upon us we are not able to educate these four millions [now more than six] of people that were turned loose among us. As I have already stated, during the period of slavery it was not our policy to educate them; it was incompatible, as we thought, with the relation existing between the two races. Now that they are citizens we all agree that it is our policy to educate them. As they are citizens, let us make them the best citizens we can. I am glad to see that they show a strong disposition to do every thing in their power for the education of their children.

Then I say the provision of the bill that gives for ten years, at least, the advantage to the States where there is most illiteracy is a just and a wise provision, and I thank the senators from New England and the other wealthier States for the sense of justice they exhibit in coming forward and showing a willingness to aid in the education of these people. We all agree that it is important that they be educated. You will agree with me that we in the Southern States are not now able to educate them and our own children. They were set free as a necessity of the Union. You so regarded it. Then it is proper that the Union should come forward, and with its vast resources aid in their education; and I am glad to see a movement made that looks in that direction.

I confess I have better hopes for the race for the future than I had when emancipation took place. They have shown a capacity to receive education, and a disposition to elevate themselves, that is exceedingly gratifying, not only to me, but to every right-thinking Southern man. And I wish you to understand that we harbor no hostility to the race in the South. There are many reasons why we should not, no good reasons why we should. They were raised with us; they played with us as children. Under the slavery system the relations were kind. When the war came on it was supposed by many that they would rise in insurrection and soon disband our armies. They at no time ever behaved with more loyalty to us, or with more propriety. Since the end of the war, when, as we thought, you very unwisely gave them the ballot, they have exercised the rights of freemen with a moderation that probably no other race would have done. Therefore, I say, it is our duty in the South especially, and I think yours in the North as well, to encourage them, and, as they are now citizens, to elevate them and make them the best citizens possible.

But, as I stated a while ago, I have given you a reason why there is such a vast preponderance of illiteracy now in our section. It is not only due to the fact that we did not have the common-school systems in the Southern States prior to emancipation, but that the four millions of freedmen were added to our population as citizens, without education. Then we must appeal to you not only now, but in the future, to be liberal toward the South in aiding in the education of these people. I know there have been complaints that they may have been cheated in some instances at the ballot-box. Ignorance may be cheated anywhere. Doubtless, senators, you have seen the more ignorant class cheated in your own States. If you would guard against this effectually in the future, educate them; teach them to know their rights, and, knowing them, they will maintain them.

What Senator Brown says of the prostration of the Southern States at the close of the war goes far to explain the fact that the Southern Churches have done comparatively little in educating the emancipated negroes. The truth is, thousands of Southern whites have been utterly unable to educate their own children. With the colleges of the South since the war it has been one long struggle for existence. There is—with the exception of Vanderbilt University, founded by the liberality of a broad-minded and patriotic citizen of New York—hardly one well endowed college or university in the South. I am speaking of institutions under the care of the Church. Many of them are well officered in every respect. Among their faculties are many men who have prepared themselves for teaching by the use of the best opportunities afforded in this country and in Europe. They have nobly undertaken to help the poor young men and women of their section, and have done the very best they could, themselves battling with half pay and poverty year after year.

The worst fault of the Southern people since the war in relation to the negro's education has not been that they themselves have done so little, but that they have not more cordially cooperated with those who were able to do great things and were trying hard to do them. For one, I am sure that I might have done much that I have not done to help those to whom, in God's Providence, this work was given. But both sides, so far as rightly understanding each other was concerned, were moving in something like a London fog. God be praised, the blue sky is breaking over us all at last!

But, after all, the South has done and is doing a great deal more than some people have thought. The Report of the Commissioner of Education for 1878, the last available to me, gives us most encouraging statements. During 1878 the former slave States expended on their public schools, $11,760,251. But it is fair to state that of this amount the three "Border States," Maryland, Missouri and Kentucky, expended $5,129 393. In the public schools of the Southern States there were enrolled 2,034,946 white children, and 675,150 colored children.

The fullest single statement that I have seen of the work done by States in the education of the negroes in the South may be found in an able address delivered by the Hon. Gustavus J. Orr, LL.D., State School Commissioner of Georgia, before the National Educational Association at its meeting at Chautauqua in the summer of 1880, on "The Education of the Negro; its Rise, Progress, and Present Status." Perhaps no man in the South is more competent to state this case. Dr. Orr is trusted and honored by all who know him for his ability, learning, and conscientious fidelity to every trust. He has accomplished wonders in Georgia, in the administration of the affairs of his department, considering the limited resources at his command. Three paragraphs from Dr. Orr's address I quote here, wishing that I could reproduce the whole of his statement and argument. After stating that the public school systems of the South began their work with the "new constitutions," Dr. Orr says:

> The adoption of these constitutions marks the era of the admission of the negro, with the free consent of the white race, to the full rights of citizenship, including the rights to free education. The great moral revolution, which had been in progress for nearly two decades, was now fully accomplished. I have endeavored to show you the difficulties through which it was necessary to pass before this end could be reached. It only remains now for me to speak of educational results—of what has been actually accomplished. I may state, then, that we have made a brave beginning. While what we have done may not be anything to boast of in itself, yet, considered in the light of the surroundings, we are not ashamed of it. We have given to the negro in our constitutions and in our statutes equal educational rights. We have sought, in administering these statutes, to hold the balance evenly. I can say for myself that there is nothing in my official career of which I am prouder than the universal recognition of the truth of this statement in respect to my own administration by our colored friends in Georgia. Large numbers of our colored people have learned to read and write and to make easy calculations. They have, moreover, been taught something of the history of this great country, and of the geography of this and other lands, and of the structure of the English language. In our cities our schools are kept up from eight to ten months of the year; but in country places the terms are necessarily short, being only from three to five months. What we do, however, for one race, the same we do for the other.

Every informed man in Georgia knows that Dr. Orr is, by the justice of his administration, fully entitled to his manly boast. He had endeavored, without full success, to obtain complete statistics for the fifteen Southern States. But the following paragraph shows something of the work that has been done; moreover, it shows progress that deserves commendation and inspires hope:

> In Virginia, beginning with the year 1871, the colored enrollment for successive years was as follows: 38,554, 46,736, 47,169,

52,086, 54,941, 62,178, 65,043, 61,772, 35,768. In South Carolina the same enrollment from 1870 has been, 15,894, 33,834, 38,635, 46,535, 56,249, 63,415, 70,802, 55,952, 62,120, 64,095. In Georgia, beginning in 1871 and omitting 1872, when there were no public schools, the same record reads, 6,664, 19,755, 42,374, 50,358, 57,987, 62,330, 72,655, while in Mississippi, beginning with 1875, the same figures were, 89,813, 90,179, 104,777, 111,796. The only year for which my correspondence enables me to present the grand aggregate for the entire South was the year 1878. The attendance for this year foots up the astonishing sum of 738,164, the reports being accurate for all the States except Arkansas, Florida, and Louisiana, in which, as already stated, careful estimates were made. When confronted by a record like the foregoing, achieved in the midst of the difficulties that beset us on every side, as a friend of the colored race I thank God and take courage!

The Southern States are doing more for the "higher education" of the colored people than many suppose. Dr. Orr gives the following statements:

> Maryland appropriates $2,000 per annum for the support of a normal school for the training of colored teachers; out of the proceeds of the "Land Scrip" fund donated by Congress, Virginia gives $10,000 for the school at Hampton. South Carolina gives $7,000 to Claflin University; Georgia pays, out of her own treasury, $8,000 to the Atlanta University; Mississippi pays for the higher education of the colored youth an average of $10,000 per annum; the new constitution of Louisiana provides for the same purpose an annual appropriation of not less than $5,000, nor more than $10,000; Missouri appropriates $5,000 per annum to the Lincoln Institute, a school for the training of colored teachers.

Dr. Orr's address closes with words that the best people in the South, the people who are going to shape its future policy, heartily indorse:

> Whether they shall ever be prepared, in mass, for the intelligent, efficient, satisfactory discharge of the functions of citizenship is a question. I believe they will, in spite of the mistakes that have been committed, if the States, the general government, and the

various Christian Churches shall do their full duty in the matter. That overruling Providence which has shaped the events of the past will not abandon them, or us, if we act like true men and Christians. In view of the mode of their introduction among us, and of the condition in which they were so long kept by laws sanctioned by the representatives of the entire people, and of the manner in which their emancipation was effected, we of the South believe that the duty of providing the means of preparing them for citizenship belongs to the whole country. We ourselves, however, have a duty to perform, which we do not intend to shirk. I think I can speak for the entire South, when I say that we are determined to stand by all that has been done. They have been declared free: to this we most heartily consent. They have been admitted to all the rights of citizenship; in this we acquiesce. Our State constitutions and our laws have declared that they shall be educated; to bring about this result we will do all that in us lies.

A great and noble work has been done by Northern philanthropists for the education and uplifting of the emancipated negroes. I regret that it is not understood in the South as it deserves to be. Some mistakes that were made in the prosecution of this good work have been alluded to, but, take it all in all, such work has not often been done in any age or country. Let us look into this work somewhat, at least take a general survey of it. The aggregates are impressive; the details are deeply interesting.

It is right to say that much was done of permanent value for the education of the emancipated negroes by the United States government, through the Freedmen's Bureau. It may be true that the very best work done through this agency of the government was its contribution to the education of the new-made citizens.

Mr. Eaton gives us the names and locations of thirty-four "normal schools" for colored people; twenty-eight "institutions for secondary instruction"; fifteen "universities and colleges," one of these being in Ohio, and one in Pennsylvania; of "theological schools," either distinctively such or providing for this with other departments, there are nineteen, all but two of them being located in the South. There are three "schools of law," and four "schools of medicine." Of the normal schools, three are exclusively State institutions, as in Alabama, North Carolina, and Arkansas. At the normal schools there were, in 1878, 5,236 pupils; at the "institutions for secondary instruction" there were 5,290; at the "colleges and universities" there were 1,620; at the "schools of theology" there were 626; at the "law schools" 44; and at the "medical schools" 94. This is a good showing thirteen years after the close of the war. And Mr. Eaton shows that in all these schools the general tendency was in the line of real progress.

Let it be fairly considered by all concerned, especially by the people of the South, that Northern money, given by private individuals, by hundreds of thousands of Christian men and women, has, for the most part, founded and sustained these great enterprises for the elevation of the African race in this country. I, for one, have considered these things, and regret many prejudices I once indulged that were not justified by even the follies and blunders that have been sufficiently alluded to. I go further; many of us of the South have not taken the right pains to inform ourselves of the work that was being done in sight of us. Not long ago, one of the best-informed men in Georgia, a cultured reader of reviews and magazines and advanced books, said to me that he did not know till January, 1881, that there was such an institution as the Atlanta University. He knew that there was something in that city of that name that received money from the State, but its grade, character, appointments, history, he knew nothing of.

A little detail may be useful in stating some of the work done by Northern Christians for our colored people. Among the chief of the societies at work in the South for the help of the colored people is the "American Missionary Association." It is the work of the Congregational Church, and the people who back this society are, for the most part, the people who back the "American Board of Foreign Missions." (Let this be considered; the work of that Board is an important part of the history of Christianity in this century.) This "American Missionary Association" is carrying on 8 chartered institutions; 12 high and normal schools; and 24 common schools, in the South. In all of them are 7,207 pupils, taught by 163 teachers. The secretaries think that at least 150,000 scholars have been taught, more or less, by the pupils educated in these high schools and colleges. This work costs money—a great deal of it. Saying nothing of the hundreds of thousands invested in buildings and school property, the work of the society in the South costs considerably more than $100,000 a year.

Some ignorant people "pooh-pooh" this sort of work. They are the people who have reason to fear that the negro will get ahead.

Some of the buildings used in these schools rank with the best in the South. The Atlanta University is now using two splendid brick buildings; another, costing $40,000, is soon to be built between them. They have a far better library than most of the white colleges of the South have, and the library has an endowment of $5,000, given by R. R. Graves, Esq., the liberal New Yorker, who gave them most of their 4,000 or 5,000 volumes. How many Southern white colleges have endowments for their libraries?

Some may doubt of the work they do. The State Board of Examiners, appointed by the governor of Georgia, say, in their published reports, that the work is done thoroughly. And so it is. The studies are well graded, the majority of the pupils being in the normal course. In the regular college courses were twenty-six last year, six being in the senior class. What do they study? I copy the curriculum taken from the Catalogue for 1880, for which thanks are due President Ware. This course speaks for itself.

College Course

For admission to this course, pupils must have passed through the College Preparatory Course, or its equivalent.

The degree of B.A. is given to graduates from this course.

FRESHMAN YEAR
Greek—Xenophon's Cyropædia, *Owen*; Homer's Odyssey, *Merry*; Grammar, *Hadley*.
Latin—Livy, *Chase*; De Senectute et de Amicitia, Crowell; Grammar and Composition, *Harkness*; Greek and Roman Antiquities, *Bojesen*.
Mathematics—Algebra, *Peek*; Plane Geometry, *Bradbury*.

SOPHOMORE YEAR

Greek—Select Orations of Demosthenes, *Tyler*; Prometheus of Aeschylus, *Woolsey*. First and Second Terms.

Latin—Odes of Horace, *Chase*; Tacitus, *Tyler*. First and Second Terms.

English—Literature, *Gilman with authors*. Second and Third Terms.

Mathematics—Solid and Spherical Geometry, *Bradbury*; Trigonometry and Surveying, *Bradbury*.

JUNIOR YEAR

Greek—Gorgias of Plato, *Woolsey*. Third Term.

Latin—Cicero's Tusculan Disputations, *Chase*. Second Term.

Rhetoric—*Hill*.

Science—Natural Philosophy. *Peck's Ganot*; Astronomy, *Lockyer's*; Chemistry, *Steele*; Geology, *Dana*.

Natural Theology—*Chadbourne*.

SENIOR YEAR

Mental Philosophy—*Porter*.

Logic—*Jevons*.

Moral Philosophy—*Fairchild*.

Evidences of Christianity—*Hopkins*.

Aesthetics—Lectures On the History of Art.

Political Philosophy—Political Economy, *Wayland*; Civil Liberty and Self Government, *Leiber*.

History—History of Civilization, *Guizot*.

The normal course is formed to "meet the immediate demand for teachers," and is well adapted to this end.

I observe in the Catalogue that most of the graduates of past years are put down as teachers. What dividends on the investment—large as it is! Who can estimate the work of these teachers? Mr. B.M. Zettler, former school superintendent in Macon, Georgia, bears emphatic testimony to their efficiency.

The Atlanta University, I am informed, is not beyond other schools of similar grade under the care of the Society. Fisk University, Nashville, represents much money, much brains, and much good work. Its grade is high; its work good. And so of many others. Let us bear in mind, too, that among the trustees and patrons of this great benevolence are hundreds among the foremost Christian names in America, many of them honored throughout the Christian world.

"The Freedmen's Aid Society" is the child of the Methodist Episcopal Church. I quote here from the "Thirteenth Annual Report," Rev. Dr. R. S. Rust, Secretary:

The Society has aided in the establishment and support of the following schools, six of which have been legally chartered, with collegiate powers:

CHARTERED INSTITUTIONS.—Central Tennessee College, Nashville, Tenn.; Clark University, Atlanta, Ga.; Claflin University, Orangeburgh, S.C.; New Orleans University, New Orleans, La.; Shaw University, Holly Springs, Miss.; Wiley University, Marshall, Texas—6.

THEOLOGICAL SCHOOLS.—Centenary Biblical Institute, Baltimore, Md.; Baker Institute, Orangeburgh, S.C.; Thomson Biblical Institute, New Orleans, La.—3.

MEDICAL COLLEGE—Meharry Medical College, Nashville, Tenn.—1.

INSTITUTIONS NOT CHARTERED.—Bennett Seminary, Greensboro, N.C.; Cookman Institute, Jacksonville, Fla.; Dadeville Seminary, Dadeville, Ala.; Haven Normal School, Waynesborough, Ga.; La Grange Seminary, La Grange, Ga.; Meridian Academy, Meridian, Miss.; Rust Normal School, Huntsville, Ala.; Walden Seminary, Little Rock, Ark.; West Texas Conference Seminary, Austin, Texas; West Tennessee Seminary, Macon, Tenn.—10.

In these institutions the number of pupils taught during the year is classified as follows:

Biblical, 372; law, 23; medical, 85; collegiate, 90; academic, 220; normal, 1,100 intermediate, 217; primary, 832. Total, 2,490.

Number of pupils taught in our schools, 63,000; number taught by our pupils, more than 550,000. Amount of permanent school property, more than $250,000. Number of teachers employed this year, eighty.

This Society has expended in this work, during thirteen years, $893,918 46. Nearly every dollar came from the North.

As to the character of the work done by the schools under the care of the "Freedmen's Aid Society," it ranks with the best at work in this field. I have read all the thirteen reports; the reports improve as fast as the schools. The orators have nearly ceased to denounce slavery; they are now, at the anniversaries, beginning to discuss right vigorously and wisely the negro's freedom. But there is still some margin for "sweetness and light." At the last anniversary meeting Bishop H. W. Warren made an eloquent address, from which I take the following extracts:

> The key-note of the present condition of our work in the South is given in the following fact:
>
> On the 16th of October, 1880, Ex-Governor Brown, of Georgia, now United States Senator, stood on the platform of the new building for Clark University, in Atlanta, and publicly gave thanks to the representatives of the North for the aid given the South in the matter of education. Before him was a throng of colored people. They were sons and daughters of a race that for the first time stood facing the sunrise. Their countenances glowed with the light of a new morning. The sun that was about to rise lighted the sky with an aurora of hope soon to brighten into an immortal day. Beside him were three other governors of Georgia, the school commissioner of the State, and representatives of the enterprise and intelligence of that swiftly rising commonwealth. On the same platform were the professors, who had gone forth in the true missionary spirit from pleasant homes and friends beloved to take up a work genial only to those who were filled with the spirit of Him who left the glory of heaven for the shame of earth, who, though rich, became poor that we through his poverty might become rich. Behind him were four Bishops, one of the blood of the race to be benefited, and three representatives of a great Church of Christ, that had been pouring out its men and its money to aid in bringing light to those who sat in darkness and the shadow of intellectual and moral death. They were there in a moment of victory to lift up the banner, to raise the shout, and then hasten on to the achievement of new victories. It was in such a presence that Senator Brown said, in effect: "I want to

publicly thank you men of the North for doing what we were not able to do. We are too poor. But it needed to be done. You have done it. Its results are apparent to-day. I thank you, and pray you to continue your help."

It was one of the sublimest moments of his life. He was permitted to speak for millions and to millions. He voiced the crying needs of multitudes who could not speak for themselves, who did not even know the depths of their need. But he, who had himself come up from lowly conditions by heroic struggles, spoke the unutterable thanks of the lowly as they saw themselves rising to sublimer heights of being. He also spoke to millions of helpers who had previously heard few voices of approval for their work save those of their friends, their consciences, and their God. Few men ever speak to so many, speak for so many, and with such appreciation on both sides. It was well and wisely spoken.

The "American Baptist Home Mission" is one of the vigorous workers among the colored people of the South.

Sidney Root, Esq., of Atlanta, Georgia, a citizen of that city long before the war, held in deserved honor as a broad-minded, cultivated Christian man, is one of the trustees of "Roberts College," an institution founded and carried on by the "Baptist Home Mission," whose head-quarters are in New York. The wisdom of the society in electing Mr. Root one of its trustees is to be commended. He is an honor to Vermont, the State of his nativity, and to Georgia, the State of his adoption. I asked him to prepare me a statement of the work done by the "Baptist Home Mission." I give his answer in full:

Atlanta, Ga., February 5, 1881.

A. G. HAYGOOD, D.D.;

MY DEAR SIR: By a note from our secretary (Rev. H. L. Morehouse, D.D.) I learn that the 'American Baptist Home Mission' of New York has expended something over $200,000 for buildings, for educational purposes among the colored people of the South; about $300,000 for salaries; and about $300,000 for current expenses and for 'beneficiary students.' These sums, together with amounts contributed for permanent endowment, represent an aggregate of about $1,000,000 contributed through the Society for educational (including theological and normal) instruction among the freedmen. The management of the several institutions has generally been committed to Southern people. The institutions are—

	Pupils in 1880
Wayland, Washington, D.C..	93
Richmond, Richmond, Va..	92
Shaw, Raleigh, N. C	277
Benedict, Columbia, S.C.	140
Roberts, Atlanta, Ga.	100
Leland, New Orleans, La.	144
Natchez, Natchez, Miss.	113
Nashville, Nashville, Tenn.	232
Total	1,191

There is now an institution in Selma, Alabama, with 260 students, partly supported by the Board; and one at Live Oak, Florida, the number of students not reported.

The Secretary writes me that he will soon prepare a table showing the number of students educated in the higher studies, and their occupation as far as known to date. You will observe, however, that, including Selma and Live Oak, there are about 1,500 students being educated as preachers and teachers among the colored people, through the agency of the Baptist Home Missionary Society.

An excellent Medical College has recently been founded in connection with Shaw University, Raleigh, N.C., by a daughter of Mr. Estey, the organ builder. I think *as the matter is managed* [Mr. Root's italics] a vast amount of good must result, and I believe you will agree with me.

Sincerely,

S. Root

The Methodist Episcopal Church, over and above its great educational work among the negroes, has done incalculable good in their uplifting through its Church Extension Society, that has aided them in building many churches, and through its Missionary Society, that has helped them to sustain them. Its money expenditures in these directions have gone beyond a million of dollars.

From the senior Secretary, Rev. Dr. A.J. Kynett, I have the following facts: From 1865 to January 1, 1881, the Society donated for building churches, in round numbers, $830,000. Of the whole amount, not less than $350,000 have been expended in the Southern States, and of the $350,000 nearly $200,000 have been used for the benefit of the colored people. Of their "loan fund"—used only in loans—less than $200,000 have been in use in the Southern States, and of this amount, about $50,000 among the colored people. The Society has aided 3,068 churches throughout the country; of the whole number, about 1,600 are in the Southern States, and of the 1,600, not less than 1,000 are for the use of the colored people.

Other Churches, whose reports are not available, have done much good. And many thousands of dollars have been given by benevolent individuals, whose benefactions do not appear in any published statistics. No doubt they are recorded where they will never be forgotten.

The Presbyterians (of the North for the most part) have done a great work in the education of the negroes. Mr. Eaton reports for them, two normal schools in the South; three "institutions for secondary instruction"; one university, the Biddle, located at Charlotte, North Carolina, and one at Oxford, Pennsylvania. The Episcopalians have established two normal schools and seven schools for "secondary instruction." The Friends have one important institution in East Tennessee. The Roman Catholics have a school for colored people in Baltimore.

For myself I have reached a conclusion about this educational work among the negroes of the South *it is God's work*. Errors and mistakes being allowed, the main facts abide. Here is a small army of devoted men and women teaching these poor negroes. Millions of dollars have been invested in the work; also millions of prayers. I have studied their reports, have looked into some of their schools, and have examined no little of their work; it is full of hope and cheerful prophecy. It is high time that those who are trying to do good should have knowledge of each other. Then they would help each other. These men and women of the North who are in the South teaching the negroes could do a great deal more good if we of the South, men and women, would do our full duty to them. If, when they know us, we "improve on acquaintance" as much as some of them have improved on acquaintance after being once known by us, then in the next generation, if not before, there will be mutual admiration, with much helping of one another in every good work. And it will be to the peace of men and the glory of God. Will not this be better than mutual suspicions, heart-burnings, and other such "works of the devil?"

15

THE NEGRO AS
A MEMBER OF THE COMMUNITY

Wise men, who wish the negro well and who have the best interests of the country at heart, will not confine their attention to his
voting. It seems to me, as heretofore intimated, that his importance as a voter has been greatly exaggerated, much to his hurt. I
say this not because he is a negro, but upon the general principle
that the man is of more consequence than the voter. Voting is
not the main business of life; determining elections is not the
chief end of a man, whether of a black or of a white man. He not
only has other duties and functions to perform, but others more
important. A citizen does not render his greatest service to society
by the act of depositing a ballot, but by his right living. What is
he? What does he do? Is he a producer? Does he add any value,
material, intellectual, or moral, to the resources of his community
and of the country? Is his personal influence good? Is his family
life a salt-savor among his children and neighbors? Is the man as
well as the voter what he ought to be?

If we must stick on this ballot question, then I have this to
say, a man's real value in politics depends upon his value in the
community. Voting is, indeed, important, but it is incidental. A
man votes, we will suppose, two or three times a year, or oftener,
as the case may be. But he is a member of the community three
hundred and sixty-five days in the year. Now, what is he in the
community? Is his influence, whether it be great or small, on the

right side of morals and progress? This aspect of the question no thoughtful person can overlook, or undervalue. For it is real, practical, abiding.

The negro is a neighbor. Perhaps there is little or no intercourse between the cabin and the mansion, or between the cabin and the cottage, or even between two cabins, a white family in one and a colored family in the other. (But I do think there is more intercourse between "mansion" and "cabin" in the South than between "brown-stone front" and "garret" in the great cities.) But the negro is a neighbor all the same, and, by his very existence and presence, a power for good or evil. If we leave the higher considerations of duty, and find the lowest place for our argument—the self-interest, the mere convenience and comfort, of the dominant race—it is important that this negro, this humblest member of the community, be a good man, a man of right views, sentiments, habits, and associations. It is important to both races that their relations be not only friendly but mutually helpful and affectionate. If this negro be a bad man, with false views, corrupt sentiments, vicious habits, and evil associations, he is a constant menace to peace and good order. Neither more nor less a menace on account of his color, but a menace on account of his character.

In what ways, now, can we of the white race help our colored neighbor to be what he ought to be as a member of the community? The answer cannot be given in detail; no rules can comprehend such a subject. Much depends on circumstances of time and place, as of persons. Of one thing we may be sure—it is not in the power of legislatures, state or national, to define the class of relations and duties I am writing of, nor to secure the results that right-minded people believe to be so necessary to the well-being of society. Social problems were never solved by legislation or authority; it is not in the nature of things that they should be solved by mere power or mere law. I am not unmindful of the value and need of good laws, of laws that defend and protect men in all their rights; that encourage, and, in so far as it is possible, secure the fullest development of the best powers that are in human nature. But I am now speaking of these relations in life that are of necessity more or less beyond the reach of human laws and their sanctions; of relations in which each man must be more or less a law unto himself.

I propose this question to myself: How must I, a white man, and my neighbor, Daniel Martin, a black man, treat each other? He is my neighbor living with his family near me; he is my friend also, in whom I can trust; more, he has been a servant in my household for six full years. Daniel is a citizen; more than that, he is a man; the law made him a citizen, God made him a man. I am as much bound by eternal righteousness to deal fairly with Daniel Martin in all things, as with the worthy man and cultured Christian minister whose garden joins mine. And, let it not be overlooked, Daniel Martin is as much bound as I am to deal righteously in all the relations that bind us together. I may, because I have larger opportunity, owe more duty to him than he owes to me, but the nature of the obligation is the same.

Does any man with a particle of sense suppose that any law can provide for all the relations that exist between Daniel Martin and me? Divine law never proceeds upon this sort of literalism in statutory enactment, that every possible duty must be named and weighed and timed and measured. When human law makes the attempt it fails always. The infinitely varied adjustments of human life make mere statutory solutions of such questions impossible. And there is another reason besides the endless variety of occasions and circumstances; if it were possible to provide for every duty by statute, there would be no place left for our personal development in good conscience and moral life.

If mere laws cannot guide and restrain Daniel Martin and me, (and both of us need guidance and restraint,) how are we to manage our seemingly difficult case? Here is our first mistake; it is not a difficult case at all, except we make it so by want of sense and of a good conscience. There is no trouble whatever, provided we two men have the right spirit in our hearts; provided, also, that we have good sense in our heads. Daniel and I have just one thing to do; we must plant ourselves squarely and sincerely on the "Sermon on the Mount." On this basis we will get on with little thought or need of outside help to the end of a long chapter.

In the course of time Daniel and I will have various business relations. (There is no discount, be it observed, in the matter of "caste" for business connections. "Business is business," unless it be in teaching his children to read!) I want Daniel's muscle, his experience in a line of things, and his integrity; he wants my money, my confidence, my friendship, and now and then when he "gets in a pinch," a little "advance," or other extra help. Some day he will have something to sell that I wish to buy; I will have something to sell that he wishes to buy; and so on to the end of our natural lives. How are we to manage? Just as two white men who wish to do right would do; just as two black men who wish to do right would do. We are each to do in all our dealings with each other the fair and holiest thing. This is all there is in it. With this difference, if I wrong him, taking advantage of his ignorance, or weakness, or dependence, of any thing peculiar to his condition that gives me the advantage of him, I am all the viler for using my advantage unrighteously. It is doubly mean for the white man to wrong a negro. And this is recognized broadly in the proverbial phrase by which some superlatively despicable person is described in all parts of the South: "He is mean enough to cheat a negro."

"But," says the irrepressible one, be he Northern or Southern, "how about the social question?" This question indicates a sort of hysteria. But if you must be answered, it is easy: Daniel Martin never asks any thing of me as to social life that I am not willing to give. I respect him in his place; he respects me in my place. He is master in his house, (except when his wife gets the upper hand,) I am master in mine, (all exceptions understood.) No test that brought embarrassment to me or mortification to him ever occurred, or ever will. Wise people never make these issues; they do not come up spontaneously, not once in a thousand times. In his capacity as servant, Daniel Martin will make fires, clean shoes, and do other such things. Were I living in New York or London, and Daniel were what he is, or any other man in similar relations to me, I should expect him to do the same things, so long as they are included in our bargain, and he is paid for his work. But I do not ask him to sit at the table with my guests, or to entertain company in the parlor after tea: He does not wish such association. *Ask him.* He has just about the same social recognition in my house that a man of all work has in other decent and well-ordered households.

There never was a subject so much discussed that has so little in it, except it may be the invention of perpetual motion. It gives no trouble to either race when left alone. People of good sense, good breeding, and of unmeddlesome temper, do let it alone.

Let us consider, as they are related to our present argument, the whole class of negroes in a community. Owing to their antecedents, (and let us remember the antecedents that are back of American slavery, antecedents that carry our thoughts back to the huts and *kräals* of Africa,) and owing also to their present circumstances, there are some lines in which they need special instruction, training, encouragement, building up. I may indicate some of them, too obvious to need elaborate discussion. I must teach the negro to respect my rights; I do this best by respecting his. I must teach him to respect and keep his contracts; to do this I must respect and keep mine. I must teach him to obey law and to respect authority; to do this I must set him the example. I must teach him to "rule well his own house"; to do this I must show him, not simply teach him, how. I must teach him to speak the truth; to do this I must speak the truth to him. I must teach him honesty; to do this I must be honest. I must teach him purity in his own life and in all his family relations; to do this I must let him see that I respect and keep the law of chastity. I must teach him the sin and ruin of drunkenness; to do this I must keep the demon from my own lips and from my house. I must teach him the sanctity of a freeman's ballot; to do this I must myself vote as an honest man upon my conscience, only for good men, only for good measures, neither buying nor selling votes, nor cheating in any way, by terror, by violence, by "ballot stuffing," by false counting, by false returns, or by any method known to demagogues of any land or race.

Some duties and virtues need emphatic, distinct, repeated, and careful statement in my efforts to do him good. For example: The negro race in the South I know, and every-where else I suppose, needs building up in all the sanctities of family life. Their slave history was not favorable to the development of right views and sentiments on this subject; it was very unfavorable to it. Nor was slavery favorable to the virtue of the white race; it was far otherwise. It was a great shame and sin that the law did not recognize their marriage relations; that it not only did not protect them from arbitrary separations, but that it did not forbid them voluntary separations. The old system worked badly for the negro, as to his conceptions of the dignity and sanctity of marriage in two directions. First, it did not forbid masters to separate husband and wife. Once in my life I saw a husband and wife "sold apart." It was long ago, in my childhood; it froze my soul with horror. But let the truth be spoken in justice to the old masters; the great majority of them would not separate husbands and wives; there was a strong sentiment against it; and the professional "negro-trader" was a man whose business was against all the sentiments of the better class of people; to many he was simply odious. Second, the old system operated badly in not compelling them to keep their marriage contracts. This was really worse for their morals than separation by sale or other form of force. Their ideal of marriage might have been elevated if separations had occurred only by outside and arbitrary power; it could not be much elevated when the law allowed them to follow their own whims and affinities.

But there was among them, in the days of slavery, and is today, a much higher average of conviction, sentiment, and practice in their marriage relations than hasty observers or careless generalizers have supposed. Many writers, arguing from the want of law to prevent masters from separating husbands and wives, and the want of law to compel them to keep their own contracts, have concluded that there was no marriage among them worth the name. This is a mistake and an injustice both to the ex-master and to the ex-slave. The one was not so heartless, the other not so debased, as has been assumed. For, 1, as has been stated, the majority of masters did not separate husbands and wives; 2, natural affection, religious principle, and the example of the white people, (there was hardly a divorce in the South till after the war,) went far to counteract in their own minds the tendency to "easy divorce."

Nevertheless, much of right teaching and training remains to be imparted. Many Southern people are truly awake to this. Moreover, the civil law enters their family life now. Their marriages must have the sanction of law; their infidelities are punishable by law. Granted that the law is not always enforced for marital infidelities, yet it is often enforced, and its tremendous educating power has fairly begun to show its benign influence. If now the Southern people only have sense and principle enough to keep out of their statute books the "easy" and unscriptural divorce laws that have already brought such harvests of shame and crime to some other sections of our country, another generation will witness vast amendment among the negroes in their conjugal and family life. But Heaven save us from these divorce laws that, in some States, have allowed one divorce to every fourteen marriages! Such laws are hardly as good conservators of marriage as was slavery itself.[1]

If we of the South are to make progress with our problem, if we are to become the people Providence designs us to be, if we are to do our duty to God and man, then let us understand distinctly, once and for all, that in the administration of law the negroes shall receive, not only in theory but in practice, fair dealing and justice. And this principle must assert itself in every court and in all matters that are brought into court. In theory we have one law for both races; the practice must be according to the theory. When the court says, Make the negro pay his debt, let it say also, The white man must pay his debt. Let the same law be applied in all criminal prosecutions. The law does not know color or condition in its definitions; the administrators of law should not know color. A crime that should imprison or hang a negro should imprison or hang a white man. When some two years ago[2] a white

---

[1] See Note at end of chapter.

[2] Written in 1881.

man, —————, of Floyd County, Georgia, was hung for the murder of a negro, it was a contribution to right sentiment and good morals in the whole State.

This is every man's question and every woman's question, for the right administration of law depends largely upon public sentiment. It is a sort of maxim that a law greatly in advance of public opinion cannot be enforced. Therefore I say this, it is every one's question. What each man and woman thinks on these subjects has much to do with the administration of justice.

I am not one of those who count it patriotic to deny what enemies or prejudiced critics charge upon us, if the facts are against us. I do not feel called on to go into any comparative statistics of crime in the different sections of our country. But this I do know, whatever may be true of other sections, there is a disgraceful and appalling amount of crimes against life in the South. Human life is held cheap. No honest and informed man will deny it. Murders are frightfully frequent, acquittals are ruinously common. There is but one remedy, the prompt, certain, rigid, and impartial enforcement of our excellent laws.

Let us remember always, we must base all our instructions and regulate all our dealings, with the black man as with the white man, upon the eternal principles of righteousness which are laid down in the word of God. The negro's ethical education, as must be the white man's, if it is to form his character and control his life, must be according to the truth as it is in the Holy Scriptures. Dr. Andrew Peabody has truly said in one place, "The Bible is the educator of civilized man."

If white people and, black people wish to know how to treat each other in all the relations of life, let them study the Bible. Take, for example, the business relations of life, the old question of capital and labor, of service and wages. For the settlement of all questions that grow out of these relations the laws laid down and the principles taught in the Bible are worth all the "political economies" in the world. They apply to all races and conditions of men, in all countries and in all times. They are as needful and useful in New England factories as on Southern plantations. Free negroes are not the only underlings in the world, negro servants are not the only hirelings. There are thousands of factory operatives, day laborers, domestic servants, mechanics, sewing women, clerks, apprentices, and such like, whose cry for justice against oppression goes up to heaven by day and by night. "For which things sake," in all lands, "the wrath of God is come upon the children of disobedience." Let us here recall some of these half-forgotten laws; they must do us all good. I know they are needed in the South; I am persuaded that they are needed wherever there are masters and servants.

A few passages will answer here; a reference Bible will show others plenty. "Thou shalt not defraud thy neighbor, neither rob him: the wages of him that is hired shall not abide with thee all night until the morning." Servants must be paid according to the promise of the bargain, their wages are their all; to hold them back because they are helpless is both tyranny and robbery. Here is another law of God in Moses; "Thou shalt not oppress a hired servant that is poor and needy, whether he be of thy brethren, or of thy strangers that are in thy land within thy gates: at his day thou shalt give him his hire, neither shall the sun go down upon it; for he is poor, and setteth his heart upon it: lest he cry against thee unto the Lord, and it be sin unto thee." God forbids not robbing only, but oppression also; the poor hireling must not be ground down to a starvation price for his sweat and muscle. Prophecy pronounced its woe upon such oppressors of men: "Woe unto him that buildeth his house by unrighteousness, and his chambers by wrong; that useth his neighbor's service without wages, and giveth him not for his work." The last of the prophets threatens vengeance against the oppressor of hirelings, and grades him with the basest of criminals. "And I will come near to you to judgment; and I will be a swift witness against the sorcerers, and against the adulterers, and against false swearers, and against those that oppress the hireling in his wages, the widow, and the fatherless, and that turn aside the stranger from his right, and fear not me, saith the Lord of hosts." St. Paul lays down broadly the principle that covers all cases: "Masters, give unto your servants that which is just and equal; knowing that ye also have a Master in heaven." St. James pierces the very marrow of all oppressors of laborers and of the helpless: "Behold, the hire of laborers who have reaped down your fields, which is of you kept back by fraud, crieth: and the cries of them which have reaped are entered into the ears of the Lord of Sabaoth." And this Lord of Sabaoth saith, "Vengeance is mine; I will repay."

There are some legal claims which, according to God's law, cannot be enforced by a good man. For instance, and it covers many cases, "No man shall take the nether or the upper millstone to pledge: for he taketh a man's life to pledge." Debts should be paid; over-exemption by law puts a premium on dishonesty; but the rich man, the well-to-do man, who strips the poor neighbor down to his skin for a debt is loathesomely mean.

That servants and hirelings should render faithfully the service due from them is taught with equal clearness. This principle covers every case, the highest and the lowest, of what is due from the servant, from the one working for wages: "Servants, be obedient to them that are your masters according to the flesh, with fear and trembling, in singleness of your heart, as unto Christ; not with eye-service, as men-pleasers; but as the servants of Christ, doing the will of God from the heart; with good will doing service, as to the Lord, and not to men."

For masters and servants, for employers and *employés*, for capitalists and laborers, God's word lays down plain and unmistakable principles that will conserve all the true interests of all men. But it is noteworthy that more is said to the master than to the servant; perhaps because the very weakness and dependence of the servant is some protection against the temptation to neglect his work—*he must*. But power in all its forms is exposed to nearly all possible forms of temptation. And God, who knows the heart, gives most warnings to those who need them most.

If we will keep these laws, interpreting and applying them in the spirit of the Sermon on the Mount, the problem is solved. Outside the principles of these laws and the spirit of the Gospel there is no solution now or henceforth. The sooner we understand this the better for all concerned. To a class of persons, to some calling themselves "publicists," "political economists," "philosophers," and to a class of so-called "reformers," and to "doctrinaires" of every breed, these notions may seem to be antiquated. So with some persons Bible morality is antiquated. But the Bible, after all, gives us the true principles of sociology. Human society cannot exist, or go on at its best, or at any thing in a thousand leagues of its best, on any other basis than that which is laid down in the book which has given to us all in our civilization that is better than paganism.

Note—As a solemn warning to our law-makers to stand by the word of God in this matter of divorce, I quote some statements made in Tremont Temple, Boston, Massachusetts, January 24, 1881, by the Rev. Samuel W. Dike, of Royalton, Vermont, who delivered a notable lecture on "Facts as to Divorce in New England." Mr. Dike's lecture was one of "The Boston Monday Lectures." After giving a detailed history of divorce and of divorce laws in each of the New England States, the lecturer said: "If, now, we sum up for New England, there were in the year of grace 1878, in Maine, 437 divorces, in all but one county; in New Hampshire, 241; in Vermont, 197; in Massachusetts, 600; in Connecticut, 401; and in Rhode Island, 196: making a total of 2,072, with one county (Androscoggin, Me.) unreported, and a larger ratio in proportion to the population than in France in the days of the Revolution. In France the ratio of separation to marriages latterly is about 1 to 150; in Belgium, of divorce to marriages, 1 to 270, with a few separations; and in England, of petitions for both divorce and separation, 1 to 300. On the basis of population by the present census, there was 1 divorce to every 819 inhabitants in Maine; 1 to about 820 in Penobscot County, the seat of a theological seminary; 1 to every 1,443 in New Hampshire; 1 to every 1,687 in Vermont; 1 to every 2,973 in Massachusetts; 1 to every 1,553 in Connecticut; and 1 to every 1,411 in Rhode Island. But no State is likely to have a larger divorce rate than Massachusetts, unless the laws and discussion speedily check the evil. But the Catholic marriages are, in four States, 27 per cent. of the whole. Assuming, which is very nearly true, that there are no divorces among these, the ratio of divorces to marriages among Protestants is 1 to 11.7 for the four States together; it being 1 to 15 in Massachusetts, 1 to 13 in Vermont, 1 to 9 in Rhode Island, and 1 in less than 8 in Connecticut.

"But what of divorce in the West? Has not this practice, in going West with the New Englander, run into greater extremes? Few States, if any, west of Ohio collect statistics of divorce. In Ohio the ratio for many years averaged 1 to 25, and now it is about 1 to 18. Indiana has changed her laws for the better; while Illinois has, it is said, adopted better forms of procedure. No city has had a worse reputation in divorce than Chicago. Yet the records of Cook County, with a population of about 600,000, for the five years, 1875–1879, show a ratio of divorce suits begun to marriage licenses taken out of 1 to 9.4. But for the year 1875 it was found that one fifth of the petitions heard were denied. Making this allowance—and the more strict practice of later years fully justified it—the ratio becomes 1 to 12. Chicago is not as bad as Hartford or New Haven."

16

THE NEGRO AND THE LAND

Unfortunately for all, the rich and the poor, the powers that be began thinking seriously on the "land question" in Ireland a few centuries too late for their peace. Had they known two or three hundred years ago what they know to-day, they would have managed better. Then might there have been a "lengthening of their tranquility." Is it not the part of wisdom for the people of the South—may be the question might be widened in its application—to take this "land question" in hand while it is still manageable?

It is not a subject to be dismissed with a sneer or a snarl. Sneers and snarls never change facts. Here are two facts: 1. There are now over six millions of negroes in the Southern States. They will some day be ten millions, and many more; the mass of them are here to stay. 2. They do and they will, of necessity, sustain some relation to the land.

If we begin in time, and employ good sense, we of the present generation may do much to make their relation to the land a useful and happy one. On the other hand, if we wait too long—missing our best opportunities—and act foolishly, we will hand down to our children an inheritance of embarrassments, burdens, and troubles without end.

We have been dealing; in a tentative sort of way, for fifteen years with the questions that grew out of emancipation, but we have done next to nothing toward a satisfactory adjustment of the relation of the freedmen to the land. Some do not seem to know that there are relations to be adjusted—they just go on the same way, from year to year, till they die. Axle-deep in ruts, they neither learn nor forget.

As a rule each year among us is experimental. As a class the land owners of the South have absolutely no defined policy. Every year we make a sort of "trial trip." Possibly all this experimenting has been for the best; certainly it could not be otherwise. We had to learn—whites and blacks alike. Neither the land owners nor the negroes could take any other land system bodily and transfer it to Southern fields. The English system, even if it suited the English, might fail utterly in the South—a large, thinly-settled country of cheap lands, with two races so singularly related in their past history and present connections. No system of any country was based on natural or social conditions like those of the Southern people. It was our equation—never yet "worked out"; we could not "copy" from another's slate; there were unknown quantities many. The time element was necessary; there was nothing we could do but make experiments to find out what best suited us.

But has not this tentative work gone on long enough? Is it not time to look beyond the coming Christmas? I ardently wish to keep to facts, and I will not affirm, but I express the opinion, that there are not in my county ten landlords or ten tenants, white or black, who have any "understanding"—to say nothing of a "contract"—that goes further than the end of this present year; and this county is much like the rest. There may be some tenants who expect to stay where they are next year; hardly any even think about the third year; but "contracts" are "for the next crop."

There are several varieties of landlord. There are the "planters," as they are called, who own large bodies of land, some few owning several plantations. For instance, a gentleman was in my office the second week in January, whose family residence is in Atlanta, Georgia. He owns, perhaps, half a dozen plantations—two or three in Alabama; he has lands in Stewart, also in Randolph, County in this State. Some of the large land owners, as, for instance, a most successful planter in Hancock County, Georgia, live upon their plantations. This gentleman owns thousands of acres, renting them to a small army of tenants, some white and some black. There is a very large class of "farmers" owning from a few hundred to a thousand acres. These, as a rule, cultivate part of their land with hired labor and rent part to tenants. White and black tenants "take land" on the same basis. Three plans, with unimportant exceptions, cover the entire tenant system among us. 1. Some lands are worked by tenants who pay "a fixed sum." Thus: A. rents, for the year, a field, or fields, to B., for so much money, B. taking the chances of the crop. It is nearly always "a lumping trade"; that is, B. does not pay so much per acre, but so much for the whole. 2. Lands are rented for part of the crop. In Georgia the tenant generally pays the landlord "one third of the corn" and "one fourth of the cotton." 3. Some combine the plans. There are many modifications growing out of side issues; as "fixing fences," "clearing lands," "furnishing fertilizers," "making advances," and many other such matters. And, as all must see, the greater the number of modifications, the larger the margin, and the more numerous the occasions for misunderstandings when final settlements are made. But in any case, with the fewest possible exceptions, it is "a one-year" system through and through. It all has to be gone over and contracted about at the beginning of each year.

The "lease" system has hardly been tried at all; it is practically unknown among us. It is, perhaps, true that hitherto the conditions of this whole question have made it impracticable to make long contracts or leases. But is this sort of thing—this everlasting flux—this annual change (or at best renewal, optional with both parties) of landlords and tenants, to go on always? Then, year by year, our difficulties and embarrassments will increase. As it seems to me, if there is no help for it, there is no help for us—whether this "us" means tenants or landlords.

Is it not time to study "leases"—long leases? If a planter is afraid to commit himself too far, might he not, while holding on to this "year-by-year" plan of renting as to a portion of his lands, try a long lease on another portion, that he may make a fair comparison of methods? People learn by trying experiments.

Is it not reasonably certain that a judicious lease system would, in the long run, be better for both parties to this question? This one-year system puts both parties in a position that landlord and tenant ought never to occupy; namely, to give as little and get as much as possible, but without reference to that which is vital to the money interests of both—the improvement of the farm. Let us see whether this is an overstatement.

1. A. rents B. for this year fifty acres, we will say, for one third of the corn and one fourth of the cotton. B. lays all his plans as to this field for this year. His thought is, I will get out of it all I can, I will put on it as little as possible, so as to save myself this year. He begins late and hurries through his year's work, so as to save, for outside jobs, all the time he can. Saving time is good, if it be not taken from the right care and culture of the land. The tenant's motive to make the land permanently better is, by this one-year plan, reduced to the lowest possible force; in many cases it is obliterated. An example occurred under my observation last year. A colored man owned a small field and rented, for one year only, another. He repaired his own fences; he did not touch the fences of the rented field, except to patch just enough to "turn stock." Now, that fence patched and not mended won't turn stock. On his own lands he used stable manure, looking to the second year for part of its benefit; on the rented land he employed guano, because he believed he would get all its benefit the first year. On the one-year plan the tenant does nothing he can help doing. He has little motive to take care of the place, except so far as may be necessary to secure his part of the year's crop. Drainage is neglected, fences are half mended, nothing is done for the real and permanent betterment of the land. This annual change destroys all healthful motive to substantial improvement of soil or premises.

2. The very fact of making contracts year by year introduces a feverish restlessness that is alien to the best agricultural life. The tenant is on the constant lookout for a change, taking often the barest chances for bettering his condition. Many of them spend enough time place-hunting to make a poor place desirable.

3. Under this one-year plan the landlord has little motive to make

permanent and valuable improvements. He knows not who will come next year, and feels no security that his improvements will be cared for.

4. It creates, as has been intimated, unnatural relations between landlord and tenant. Each is looking out for himself, and neither has any business interest in the other beyond the end of the year.

There are seeming exceptions to the foregoing statements concerning the prevalence of the one-year system, as in many cases where tenants or hired hands remain for a number of years, annually renewing their contracts. This is only better than an actual move and change each year, but it does not secure, as is obvious, the benefit of a long occupancy provided for in the contract. In the "state of mind," restless, uncertain, and more or less suspicious, that has prevailed with our people, both with whites and negroes, for a number of years, it may well be admitted that these year-by-year arrangements were all that were practicable. Very well; but what about the next decade, the next generation, the next hundred years? Surely no one who has informed himself on these subjects in the history of other nations, or who can look straight at disagreeable facts which involve himself, will undertake to justify on grounds of sound economy our present uncertain and wasteful system.

Let me ask if it be profitable to rent a farm to a freedman for one year for so much money, or for a part of the crop, why will it not be more profitable to rent it to him for ten years, at a somewhat lower rate? Would the landlord not realize more on a ten-years' lease to a proper tenent at one fifth of the crop than at one third paid by the same tenant during the ten years on an annually renewed rent contract, where neither party looks beyond "next Christmas?" If not, why not? It seems to me that in such a test of methods one fifth would turn out more than one third.[1]

---

[1]Improved lands and better tillage would avoid a dilemma in which an old negro of our village found himself a number of years ago. He was a long time the servant of the Rev. John W. Talley, a venerable superannuated preacher of the South Georgia Conference, of the Southern Methodist Church. His name was William, and he, too, was a preacher. He stood on his dignity beyond most of his race, and would introduce himself to strang-

The ten-years' lease would, at least, offer the tenant some inducement to improve the farm; the one-year plan only makes it to his interest to squeeze out of it all he can. The rule as stated is to put nothing on that he cannot get off by Christmas. He does not drain, he does not make a good fence, he does not plant a tree, he does not plow for next year's crop, he does not permanently enrich the lands; he does nothing in the world he can help doing, except as it effects the crop in hand. A sensible, and therefore just, lease system would save to the South millions of dollars now paid out every year for "commercial fertilizers," in which there has perhaps been as much downright swindling as in any business ever carried on among men. On our one-year plan of renting lands "guano" is necessary; there must be quick returns and the tenant wants it all returned; on a long-lease plan the more natural and permanent methods of fertilization would, beyond question, be adopted, because it would be to the interests of all to adopt it. And in due course of time it would come to pass in the South, as in other countries well tilled, the longer a field is cultivated the more productive it becomes. As things have been with us, men in buying or renting lands are influenced in their judgment very much as they are in buying a horse—the older he is the less he is worth.

It is surely time that our people began to study the lease systems of other countries; it is time to begin experiments for ourselves; in due time we will develop a system suited to our wants.

---

ers after this fashion: "Mornin', sah; I am the Rev. William Talley, sah." His face was a study, particularly the mouth, which was over-size. That indescribable "set "which so often shows itself in the lips of colored preachers—and of some white preachers, too—was in the Rev. William a striking part of the countenance. It comes through cultivating solemnity of expression, not from a hypocritical tendency, but from the belief that it is "the way to do," if one would be thought very pious. During the last year of the war, standing in the passenger depot in Atlanta one day, I heard a wicked fellow say, "I'll bet a dollar that old darky is a preacher; I know by his mouth."

On one occasion the old man was sent to "haul in" the corn crop from a little field his master had rented for "the third." The old fellow was perfectly honest, though not up in arithmetic. It turned out that the little field yielded but two loads. Old William put both loads in his master's crib, and reported to the astonished landlord as follows, "Dare is no third, sah, de land am too pore to perduce de third, sah." It was not a bad commentary on our very primitive, hand-to-mouth system of annual renting.

Some day there will be, it is to be hoped, an end of this "crop-to-crop" method of farming; leases for ninety and nine years will yet be made of Southern lands.

In concluding on this point it may be remarked that a long lease is itself a conservative influence. The longer the lease the less of a "tramp" does the tenant become. It not only settles him down to systematic, intelligent work, but it tends to deliver him from the systemless and thriftless style of living that characterizes the man who only does "jobs" as he can pick them up from day to day, and that shows itself in the life of the man and the family that always expects to "move at the end of the year."

For a long time, many of the negroes, perhaps the majority of them, will be hirelings; at most, tenants. So will be many white men. There never was a country where all were fitted to be proprietors even of very small "holdings." And for the reason it is not in them to "hold" any thing; they have no grip; If every negro family (so far as the general truth is concerned the adjective may be dropped) were to begin this year with the mythical "forty acres and a mule, and a year's supply of provisions," or with any other similar outfit for independent life as small proprietors, it would not be long before a great multitude would be landless and knocking at the doors of better managers for employment. But many negroes are fitted to be land-owners, as well as long tenants, and they will be if the chance to give to them. And it is sound policy to give them the chance—the chance to buy and pay for and own farms suitable to them.

A farm worth buying is good enough to pay for itself in a few years, if it is in the hands of a man fit to own it. I believe that, on many accounts, it is desirable that a large number of negroes should become land-owners. In looking into this subject, it will hinder clearness of judgment if we raise, prematurely, the question, If many of them become land owners, where are planters to get labor? For this discussion concerns not the planter alone, but the whole frame-work of our Southern system. This is not a question of what is to the convenience or interests of a few thousand planters, but of what is to the interests of several millions of people. I have no prejudice against that small and diminishing class known as "planters," as distinguished from "farmers." I have no reason to have. Many of my best personal friends are among them. But the welfare of the whole people is a more important matter than the welfare of a few men.

Moreover, as I think, my friend, planter A., is unnecessarily alarmed about his future labor; surely it is not necessary that the many should be kept landless that the few may secure laborers.[2]

There are several things planter A. may consider to abate his alarm. 1. There will always be a great multitude of landless people. Not before the millennium will all families have homes of their own. 2. Good wages always attracts labor. But if planter A. should fail of getting negro labor to suit his views, there are still open doors of deliverance for him. He may, (1) as most landlords do in older countries, give long leases to worthy tenants; or, (2) look to other labor; or, (3) if nothing can be done, he can sell out. For, if it come to this, it is better there should be no great planters than that there should be hundreds of thousands of landless people re-enforcing year by year the army of tramps and criminals.

Some of the benefits that would accrue to the whole people, to the State, if a large number of negro families should become the owners of their own farms, I suggest. There are others of importance that will suggest themselves to the reader—some, no doubt, that have not occurred to me.

1. Owning land tends to foster the virtues that make a people happy, strong, and prosperous. It encourages industry and promotes economy. It furnishes the right soil for all those affections and sentiments that are the life and soul of *homes*. The one-year tenant has the poorest chance to make a home; the long-lease tenant is in far better case; the land owner, although of only a very small "parcel of ground," is in the best case of all. The best homes grow out of ownership of the soil.

---

[2]If it be said, "A few men own the land in England," I answer, Yes; but their long-lease system largely satisfies the land-owning instinct of their tenants. On our year-by-year system they could not hold their land, with a crowded, clamorous population around them; and they do not feel over-secure as it is.

2. Owning land makes people, of whatever color, more conservative. This has always been true. The wisest of the Romans understood this. Land-owners are almost entirely removed from the influences of communism. Mobs are not made up of land-owners. The ownership of an acre and a cabin makes a man think twice before taking part in a riot. Is it not to be considered that six millions of landless people, moving, most of them, every year, are in position to be influenced by the fanatics and desperadoes that break out now and then in some of our cities?

3. Land-owners feel an interest in government beyond their mere chance at its disbursements. The land-owner, although of but few acres, is concerned about the income as well as the outgo of public money; he is concerned in the question of taxation. While planter A. is nursing his unnecessary fears about a lack of labor, should a goodly number of negroes become small proprietors, would it not be well for him to think of the possibilities of his being taxed out of his great estates? The landless are always tempted to overtax proprietors; and there are always demagogues plenty to speculate on this tendency. If we should live to see ten million negroes in the South, (our children will,) and nearly all of them landless, and among them two millions of voters, we will see a very unhealthful, not to say, dangerous, state of things. In such a case all landowners and property owners of every class are at the mercy of the landless multitudes, who are practically irresponsible to reason, in that their poverty exempts them from taxation and their unreasoning instinct puts the blame of their poverty on the rich minority. We may not wait two generations to realize these dangers; they may not be far off; there are now premonitory tremors in the ground. *The negro vote in the South, in a number of States at least, has been divided once by Southern men.* Many do not see the significance of this. Yet there are demagogues enough to use all the instincts of this once divided black vote to turn the scale in many elections. But if among the ten millions of negroes who will be here after a while there should be only five hundred thousand owners of farms, even small farms, there will be in them a conservative force that may save all property from virtual confiscation

and society from chaos. If planter A., with his five thousand acres, is wise, he will hasten to establish a few negro voters as land-owners. He will save money by making it to their interest to keep a sharp eye on government, its taxations, and its disbursements. If planter A. thinks it important that this colored man vote with him, he would better establish him as a proprietor. When it comes to taxes, the land votes, for the most part, one way.

4. Owning land will, in most respects at least, have the same effect upon the negro that if has upon the white man. It will create in him so deep a personal and family interest in honest and capable government, as greatly to raise his character as a voter. A man who owns a farm, be it ever so small, is not so apt to sell his vote for a dollar or a dram as is the man who owns nothing but his muscle. Such a voter begins to consider the character of the man he votes for. Bad legislation will, he sees, come back to his farm. There can be no doubt that owning even a little property, especially landed property, greatly sharpens a voter's wits, in town or country, in choosing rulers. In this one case, at least, self-interest serves to clarify the judgment and to support the conscience.

What is equally important, the man who feels that the acre he works is his own is more independent in his choice and action. We may be very sure that one hundred negroes owning little farms, and one hundred owning nothing, are very different forces in society and government. It is just as true of white men.

5. If such of them as are fitted for it were land-owners they could do something in bearing the expenses of government. They would largely increase the resources of the State. Some will say: "Somebody owns the land now and pays tax on it." But he owns, most likely, a great deal that pays him nothing and that is on the tax lists at one tenth of what it ought to be worth. Mr. B.'s plantation of one thousand acres, half worked and a burden to him, is nominally worth from $4 to $6 per acre. From what he told me recently, I doubt if it nets him three per cent. on this low nominal valuation. If five hundred of the one thousand acres were divided into ten fifty-acre farms, and worked by as many negro families, owning

them, the value of the whole would be doubled. The five hundred sold would support as many as fifty persons, and leave something to sell; the five hundred kept by Mr. B. could be put in first-class condition with part of the proceeds of the portion sold; it could be worked effectively and made worth more than the whole of the thousand acres as they now stand. There are thousands of proprietors in Mr. B.'s case, and there has been enough experimenting of the kind suggested to show its feasibility and usefulness.

Is there any property less valuable or desirable than a large landed property that cannot be worked, or in any way made productive, but that must pay tax year after year? We have multitudes of poor and embarrassed land-owners in the South who would be comparatively rich with one half of what they now own and cannot manage.

6. The South needs a large number of negro farmers, settled on their own farms, for a reason that will some day become exigent: we need them as a grand self-sustaining and efficient moral and social police against the idle and vicious of their own race. The land-owning negro is the sworn foe of "tramps." The antagonism is as natural as that between shepherds and "sheep-killing dogs." It is a very rare thing that a negro desperado belongs to a family settled on its own land. If a large number of negro families were established on their own farms they would prevent, cure, and put down vagabondage as no "vagrant act" ever devised could do it.

7. It is of very great importance to make possible such industrial and social development among the negroes that they may become strong enough to provide for the helpless of their own race. I could mention a number of cases, where the fact of owning a little land enabled certain negro families to assist others of their race, less fortunate, in the hour of their need. Within gunshot of my own house are several negro families able to make comfortable some old and helpless "grandfathers" and "grandmothers" by virtue of owning their homes. And they do it creditably to themselves; thus honoring their own hearts and keeping their poor "off the county."

Our white people may, however, make up their minds to it,

that if the negroes continue, as most of them now are, for another generation, we will have to go into the business of keeping "poor-houses" and of supporting paupers on a scale of things not now in our imagination. By every consideration of good sense and good conscience, if the negro is to stay here, (and nothing is more certain so far as human calculations go,) we should desire him to become as useful as he may be made to himself, his family, his neighbors, and the State.

8. I mention another matter of large significance and importance, that will be considered some day. May it not be too late! It is eminently desirable that the negro, as a citizen and as a man, should develop in his breast the *sentiment of patriotism*. Up till a recent period their interest in the country has been largely confined to one of the political parties. But partisan zeal is no substitute for patriotism; nor is gratitude to a party, or to a section of the country, even, a substitute for love of country. In several communities I have observed that as the negroes lost interest in the party with which they had been identified, they lost their interest in the elections, and largely in the country itself. It is absolutely certain that thousands upon thousands of negroes did for years stand in expectancy, looking for the "forty acres and a mule." And it is equally certain that this foolish deception went far to shake their confidence and to disgust them with politics.

There is, I believe, no condition so favorable to the development of patriotic feeling among a people with the antecedents and surroundings of Southern negroes as the ownership of land. In every nation patriotism is rooted in the soil and nourished by it.[3]

---

[3]It is proper and just to say that one strong reason, alluded to in chapter ii, why many Southern people have been reluctant to sell lands to negroes, is their fear that it might retard the immigration they hope for. They feel, what all the world knows, that slavery formerly, and the presence of free negroes now, with all the embarrassments that have grown out of these facts, have been a bar to immigration. Witness the fact that there are in Georgia, for example, in a population of 1,538,783, only 10,310 of foreign birth. But I suggest that the foreigners who might wish to come among us would prefer to settle in a State where many of the negroes own farms than where they own none; simply because all men, who think clearly, must know that a land-owner, though poor and black, is a better citizen and a better neighbor than a man who changes his place, or is liable to

9. I mention, lastly, as a reason why it is desirable that there should be many land-owners among the negroes what good people will consider and lay to heart: it is best every way for their moral, social, and race development. I cannot conceive of a good man who does not wish the best fortune to all men of every race. I cannot conceive of a good man who would not rejoice to see the negroes more comfortable, intelligent, moral, useful, than they are. I should despise myself to have any other feeling toward any human creature. And let us remember always that in thinking of the providence of God, in his dealings with the negroes in this country, we must never confine our thoughts to those few negroes nor to this small section of the earth. We must think of the unknown millions in Africa and of the destiny of two continents. That the Christianized negroes in this country may realize their providential mission in the world, they have need to be anchored in the soil that supports them. For the Church no less than the State must, in the last analysis, find its resources of men and money in agriculture. The field and not the counting-room is at the basis of society. Africa must largely draw its missionary re-enforcements, generation after generation, from the land-owning negroes of the Southern States of our Union.

---

change it, every year. I undertake to say, and with perfect confidence, that the negroes who, in Georgia, according to the Report of the Comptroller-General for 1880, own 586,664 acres of "improved lands," represent the very best sense and character in the negro population in the State.

17

THE AFRICAN CHURCHES IN AMERICA

I have said that there are nearly one million people of African blood communicants in the different Churches in this country.[1] The whole negro population has been brought largely under the influence of religious principle and sentiment.

I have had good opportunity to know the religious characteristics of these people. My old nurse, "Aunt Esther," was a Christian, if ever there was one in this world. She lived and died in the enjoyment and practice of religion. Her plaintive melodies linger in my grateful memory to this hour. My mother has with her now the same cook she had in 1851. "Aunt Mary" is a "stalwart Methodist"; the pictures of all her Bishops, Bishop Allen's in the center, hang in her room. She shouted mightily the first time she listened to my boy-preaching, in 1858, while yet a student in Emory College.

I have seen the negroes in all their religious moods, in their most death-like trances and in their wildest outbreaks of excitement. I have preached to them in town and city and on the plantations. I have been their pastor, have led their class and prayer meetings, conducted their love-feasts, taught them the Catechism.

---

[1] I might have said more than a million, as follows—those "estimated" expressing the judgment of the best informed:
- African Methodist Episcopal Church: 214,808
- Methodist Episcopal Zion Church, (colored): 190,000
- Colored Methodist Episcopal Church: 112,300
- Meth. Episcopal Church (col'd members estim'd): 300,000
- Colored Baptists (estimated): 500,000

I have married them, baptized their children, and buried their dead. In the reality of religion among them I have the most entire confidence, nor can I ever doubt it while religion is a reality to me. Their notions may be in some things crude, their conceptions of truth realistic, sometimes to a painful, sometimes to a grotesque, degree. They may be more emotional than ethical. They may show many imperfections in their religious development; nevertheless their religion is their most striking and important, their strongest and most formative, characteristic. They are more remarkable here than anywhere else; their religion has had more to do in shaping their better character in this country than any other influence; it will most determine what they are to become in their future development. No man, whatever his personal relations to the subject, who seeks to understand these people, can afford to overlook or undervalue their religious history and character. Whatever the student of their history may believe on the subject of religion in general and of their religion in particular, this is certain—it is most real to them. To them God is a reality. So are heaven, hell, and the judgment-day.

Their Churches are the centers of their social and religious life. No man has more influence with his following than has the negro pastor. Some of their "shepherds" may be far from being "patterns and ensamples to the flock," but they have power with their people. Many of them are men who, in zeal, devotion, and Christlikeness of spirit, are worthy to take rank with the confessors and saints of any age or Church. There is an old man in this village from whom the wisest may learn and the holiest may receive new inspiration in their religious life. Many times he has done me good. David Cureton will claim many stars in his crown of rejoicing. In the old days many of the slave preachers were men of marked character and religious power. Many will be their trophies when "the day" reveals the secrets of all men. Their skill in "exegesis" and "dialectics" was limited, but their power in exhortation and application was notable.[2] Now that education is

---

[2] The following incident is historic. I suppress his name, for I truly respect him, and somebody might tease my old colored brother. He was preaching on the "Fiery Furnace

doing its blessed work in them more perfectly, many of them are men of real intellectual power. Some names could be given that are known and honored on both sides of the Atlantic.

The hope of the African race in this country is largely in its pulpit. The school house and the newspaper have not substituted the pulpit, as a throne of spiritual power, in any Christian nation. I do not believe that they ever will. But for this race the pulpit is pre-eminently its teacher. Here they must receive their best counsels and their divinest inspiration. I say *its* pulpit; I mean this. White preachers have done much and ought to have done more; they can now do much and ought to do a hundred-fold more than they do; but the great work must be done by preachers of the negro race. Tongues and ears were made for each other; in each race both its tongues and its ears have characteristics of their own No other tongue can speak to the negro's ear like a negro's tongue. All races are so; some missionaries have found this out. In every mission field the "native ministry" does a work that no other can do.

How urgent the need and how sacred the duty of preparing those of this race whom God calls to preach to their people! Heaven bless the men and women who have given money and personal service for their education! Heaven bless their "schools of the prophets!" May they ever be under the wisest guidance and the holiest influences!

Mistakes were inevitable; some unwholesome influences have, in some cases, marred the good work. This should not surprise us. But, after all, never was money better spent than in founding

---

and the Three Hebrew Children." His history and geography were confused, and by some chance he got his biblical history mixed up with some mythologic nonsense he had heard from the "college boys." He gave a most dramatic account of the scene and occasion—they excel in this sort of thing—and managed himself and his theme tolerably well till he came to speak of the "fourth" man whom Nebuchadnezzar saw "walking in the midst of the fire." Whereupon he delivered himself in this wise: "My brutherin, commontators differ as to who this fourth one wus. Some say it wus Moses, some say it wus Isaiah; but my opinion is he ware Jupiter." Yet this same man had power with men in exhortation and power with God in prayer. On questions of sin, repentance, faith in Christ, and religious experience he could touch the conscience till it quivered in agony, and move the heart till it melted with contrition or burst forth into songs of gladness, Moreover, he lived his religion.

training-schools for a native African ministry. Would God that some Southern men and women counted themselves worthy to take part in this ministry of consecrated gold and holy teaching!

I am as sure as I am that it is January, 1881, that the negro preachers are, as a class, improving, and that they are capable of large culture, both intellectual and spiritual. But I do not wish to theorize about their intellectual capacity—overestimated by enthusiasts, on one side, underestimated, on the other, by those who think that consistency means sticking to an expressed opinion, facts or no facts. The measure of their capacity I do not know; perhaps no man knows. How should any one know? The experiment is only in process; it may take a century to complete it. But nothing is more certain than that they are capable of large improvement.

In studying the religious characteristics of the negroes one who is informed and is only concerned about facts—leaving his theories and pet plans of Church work to take care of themselves—will be impressed with the power of their ecclesiastical organizations. Whether the negro Church leaders have an instinct for government I know not, but this I know—they hold together well. They are devoted to their Churches. There is not simply individual enthusiasm, but a certain *esprit* in the congregations that might well be the envy and despair of many a white pastor. They go their length for their Church. But one Church in the world has such a grasp upon the money question—I mean the Roman Catholic Church. A negro congregation in Atlanta, for instance, (where I recently, after preaching in one of the colored churches, witnessed a collection that was a marvel to me;) will raise more money, in proportion to ability, than any white congregation in that city of enterprise and liberality. When two of the "stewards," appointed to this office, stand up before the chancel and take up the collection, the contributors marching up while the congregation sings some simple recitative and chorus of their own, then, be sure, there will be a hail of nickels and dimes. They work wonders in their money management—particularly the "stewardesses." To mention another characteristic, no people in the world can match them in sticking to a protracted meeting. It is no uncommon thing for them to hold straight on for three or even six months. There is something in this persistence besides religious enthusiasm; the Church, as intimated above, is the center of their social as well as of their religious life. In any view, it is a potent influence. No doubt there are many follies and extravagances, many mistakes and wastes of power, but, nevertheless, they make headway.

The most remarkable tendency that has so far shown itself in the development of their ecclesiastical life is the strong, and, as I think, resistless, disposition, in those of like faith, to come together in their religious organizations. The centripetal is stronger than the centrifugal force. We have already a number of African Churches. Indeed, the great majority of them belong to Churches not only of their own "faith and order," but of their own "race and color." This tendency showed itself in many ways in the South, before their emancipation. I have known them, in old times, walk from ten to fifteen miles on a Sunday to attend their own meetings. This disposition has become very pronounced, and has expressed itself on a very large scale since they were set free.

I have meditated much on this subject, and give my opinion—holding it subject to revision, if the facts of their future development require it. As the matter appears to me, after much observation and much conversation with those who fairly represent their people, there is somewhere, in their secret thoughts and aspirations, a mighty under-current of sentiment that tends to bring them into race-affiliations in their religious development. It is an instinct that does not recognize itself, that does not argue, that cannot express itself in words, but that moves straight on to its ends, steady, resistless, and, in the end, triumphant. And, as this whole problem appears to me, the hand of God is in it. He who gave to the stork knowledge of "her appointed times" in her flight through the heavens, has implanted this strong instinct of coming together, and for the wisest and most beneficent of far-reaching and saving ends.

An illustration is now being furnished of the correctness of these views, and in a very impressive and striking manner. The Methodist Episcopal Church is, perhaps, the strongest single ecclesiastical organization in this country. Since the war this

Church has lavished—and not always wisely—its treasures of men and money upon the South. Its disbursements of money in the prosecution of its Southern work sum up among the millions. We have seen what it has been doing for thirteen years through the "Freedmen's Aid Society." Its great Missionary Society has spent hundreds of thousands upon their Southern work. The "Church Extension Society" has helped mightily—investing many thousands in assisting the negroes to build churches.

Within the old slave States they have about 400,000 members. Of the whole number perhaps 250,000 are negroes. In such States as Virginia, the Carolinas, Georgia, Alabama, Mississippi, and Louisiana the negroes are very greatly in the majority.

I have had good knowledge of the work of the Methodist Episcopal Church in the South. I have studied the subject carefully in their broad exhibit of statistics and in their press. I have studied it also in detail. In my town of Oxford they have a church. Some of its members are of my house-hold. Among its older members are those who were members of the Methodist Episcopal Church, South, before the war. I was, with the Rev. John W. Talley, at one time, in 1859, their pastor. The old college janitor, the Rev. David Cureton, now a superannuated preacher of the Savannah Conference of the Methodist Episcopal Church, was a local preacher in the old organization. "Judge Levi," and "Mrs. Judge"—as they were known to the students—who lived near the college campus thirty years ago, where they live to-day, were members then and they are members now. In this congregation is the quadroon woman, "Aunt Amie," or Mrs. Williams, (she that has "had her own time and her own way" for thirty years,) who will be remembered by many old students for excellent laundry work. And others of the "old set" still survive—much inclined they are to look upon the younger negroes, who never knew the "old times," as mere *parvenus*. In their social and religious character they are as good as the new, and as workers somewhat better. Faithful work was done for them, and the colored pastors of to-day will not take it to heart if it be suggested that the preaching in the old time averaged better than it does now.

Since this Church, with many others, "went over" in a body to the Methodist Episcopal Church, in 1867, I have had exceptionally good opportunity to know their affairs. My honored father-in-law, the Rev. John W. Yarbrough, of blessed memory, who was an itinerant (and ordained elder by Bishop Morris) before the "division," who had been from 1844 a traveling preacher in the Church South, entered the ministry of the Church North, January, 1867. After seven years of faithful service in the Church North, he returned to the Church South, and having, in both Churches, diligently "served his generation according to the will of God," winning many trophies in each, died, December 16, 1879, in the fullness and triumph of Christian faith. He was for two years the pastor of this Oxford Colored Church in their present organization, and for four years their presiding elder. From him I learned all the facts that characterized their transition period, and whatever was important in the opinions and sentiments of the other colored Churches in his charge.

For six years and more I have had my residence very near their Church, preaching for them and helping them in all ways possible to me.[3] I was welcomed by them before the "Cape May Treaty" between the two Churches.

I think I know the Oxford Colored Church well. My opinion is, it is steadily improving, being yet far from perfection. For years the Freedmen's Aid Society helped to support a school for them. It was while on an official visit to this school that I first met the Rev. Dr. R. S. Rust, the Secretary of the Society, and began to learn something of their methods. In this school many have been taught the "rudiments," and so the average intelligence has increased. I have known their pastors, who, for several years past, have been colored men. Some of them have been very ignorant, some of them rather superior for their class. But this is certain, they improve. This Church "commands better talent" than it did six years ago. One of its dangers is, and it is no small danger,

---

[3]Some of the more "stylish" have imitated white people, going from their pastor for exceptional service, as a marriage or a funeral, and have insisted on my presence. But the colored pastors have not seemed to be at all jealous; the "fees" disturb no man's equanimity.

nearly every man among them who feels that he has some "gift of speech" wants "license." As many white Churches have done, they, too, have overdone the "license" business, sometimes mistaking, I have thought, a desire to do good for a call to preach.

The reader will pardon these rather gossipy details. I wished to show that I have not been looking at these people through a telescope, that I have some right to an opinion as to their characteristics and tendencies.

Now, the Methodist Episcopal Church has done very nearly its best for these colored people in the South, and its best means a great deal. And the colored people are not ungrateful. This Church has not only spent millions of money, it has laid itself out to make the colored members "feel at home." They began with mixed Conferences, not distinguishing colors in statistics or appointments. Of eloquent speech and writing there has been no lack to educate the colored people to forget their color. This tenderness shows itself even in the "Discipline," and in a way certainly amusing and probably embarrassing. Thus paragraph 396 reads, "Blue Ridge Conference shall include the State of North Carolina." This is the white Conference. Paragraph 444 reads, "North Carolina Conference shall include the State of North Carolina not included in the Blue Ridge Conference." This is the colored Conference. A high official of the Church says frankly: "This clumsy form of speech is fetched about to avoid any specific allusions to color." He thinks it "over-fastidious." But it illustrates how earnestly this great Church has sought to cause itself and to cause the negroes to forget color. Nothing in the range of reason has been left undone to accomplish this result. The experiment has been made fully, vigorously, patiently, and by leaders wise in managing men.

But nature asserts herself. In nearly all of the States the Conferences are now unmixed; in all of them where the negroes are sufficiently numerous to form separate organizations. As oil and water diligently shaken together in a vessel mix for a time, but without chemical union, so these two races mixed in the Conferences for a time. When the mixture settled, lo! the oil and the water touched, but were distinct.

People who build theories out of facts will study such a case as this.

Why this unmixing? At whose instance? Not at the instance of the white preachers, most certainly. They were committed, by every form of words, to the opposite view. Indeed, every body knows the white preachers did not drive them off. (But after the experiment had gone on for some years they were, I am inclined to believe, "resigned" to the separation into "two bands.")

But instinct is supreme; the colored brethren were restless till they had their own Conferences. It was the same instinct, for instinct it is, that led to the formation of a number of African Church organizations in the North long ago. The Methodist Episcopal Church, South, recognized (quite resignedly, I must allow) this instinct, and in 1870 erected their colored members into a separate ecclesiastical organization,—"The Colored Methodist Episcopal Church in America." It is an immense name, but the shorter ones had been appropriated. This colored Church has wrought famously during the ten years of its existence, numbering in 1880 112,300 members. The Discipline of this Church, by the way, expressly provides that no white man can become a member. One white man desired admission into one of their Conferences, and was refused.

The Baptist negroes, also, like globules of mercury, have run together. So of the rest, where there have been numbers large enough.

It is this instinct that has called upon successive General Conferences—and that will continue to call—for "a colored Bishop." I have talked with many of their preachers and laymen to find out, if I could, what is the very truth in this call. Their earnestness is out of all proportion to their arguments; their logic is not at all equal to their feeling in the matter. Hence logic does not satisfy them when the Conference declines their request. The Conference follows its logic as well as its feeling—should I say instinct?—and declines; the colored brethren follow their feeling and brace its cry by such logic as they can master. They do not see very clearly how a colored Bishop is to be more useful; they know well that, in some respects, a white Bishop can do more for them;

they cannot, to their own satisfaction, quite make out their case. But they want their colored Bishop all the same.

Their arguments wont stay answered; as well argue with magnetic currents. Instinct never yet surrendered to arguments; it is their race-instinct, deep and strong and "inexpugnable," as Carlyle would say. Who that heard their impassioned speeches at Cincinnati, in May, 1880, could doubt that their appeal came, not from the cold conclusions of the reason, but red-hot out of their hearts, from the irresistible promptings of instinct? Listening to their speeches, I felt strongly the mighty under-current that their words but feebly revealed and I felt—"They are right; they do well to ask this Conference for a Bishop of their own race." Listening to the words of the white leaders of the Conference, and looking at the subject in the light of cold judgment, I said to myself, "This Conference is also right to decline the request."

This instinctive disposition to form Church affiliations on the color basis maybe wise or unwise. But it is in them—deep in them. The tendency is strengthening all the time. This instinct will never rest satisfied till' it realizes itself in complete separations. Whether we of the white race approve or disapprove matters little. The movements that grow out of race-instincts do not wait upon the conclusions of philosophy; nor do they, for a long time, take counsel of policy. We may, all of us, as well adjust our plans to the determined and inevitable movements of this instinct—that does not reason, but that moves steadily and resistlessly to accomplish its ends. It is a very grave question to be considered by all who have responsibility in the matter: Whether over-repression of race-instincts may not mar their normal evolution—may not introduce elements unfriendly to healthful growth—may not result in explosions? I have seen a heavy stone wall overturned by a root that was once a tiny white fiber. Instinct is like the life-force that expresses itself in life—or in death.

But, so far as the duty of the white race is concerned, what would it matter if all the colored Christians should segregate into Churches of their own color as well as their own faith? Nothing whatever. No right-minded Church can wish to hold on to them for mere aggrandizement in numbers; for displays in the "Year-Books" of statisticians; or for any other reason "of the earth earthy." Such "numbering of Israel" is not of the spirit of Christ. With David's example before us we should "crucify" this sort of "carnal ambition."

If every colored Methodist in the United States were to-day in one organization, this would not change the grounds or nature of our obligations to them in any respect, so far as fraternal love, fraternal aid, and co-operation are concerned. It would then, as now, be our duty to help them in all possible ways; and, considering their history in this country, and the providential indications of their relation to the salvation of Africa, just as much our duty then as now. It does not lessen the interest and love of a right-minded mother in her daughter when that daughter becomes a mother and keeps her own house. If there be any difference, the mother is more of a mother when she becomes a grandmother.

If there were not one negro in the Methodist Episcopal Church the "Freedmen's Aid Society" would be as much needed as it is now. The "Colored Methodist Episcopal Church of America" that was "set up"—I hope not "set off"—needs the help of its mother, the Methodist Episcopal Church, South, every whit as much as if they were still with us. Nay—all the more because they are not with us.[4] And we ought, before God, to help them. If any think that setting them up, or off, was only getting rid of a burden, let them repent of this evil thought—for evil it is, as sure as the stars shine.

So if all the Baptist, or Presbyterian, or Congregationalist, or other colored Christians, should come together in Church organizations of their own color only, in white Baptists, Presbyterians, Congregationalists, or others, would still be under sacred bonds to help them in every good word and work. This I lay down as

---

[4]The next General Conference of the Methodist Episcopal Church, South, should take vigorous action to establish a great "training-school" for this colored daughter. If God spares his life, Dr. John B. M'Ferrin is the man to take the matter in hand and put it through. This note is on my own long-meditated thought. The doctor knows not that I write it, nor any other.

fundamental and vital—if we are ever to do clear thinking on the subject, or to discharge our duty to God in them, it will never do to make our religious interest in the negro depend upon his being a member of our particular Church organizations. We can't throw off our responsibilities by ceasing to "count" him; nor can we measure our duty by his relation to our statistical glories and greatness.

At this point, as well as elsewhere, I wish to say—because it ought to be said—of Southern Christians as a class: They are in a state of mental unrest as to their present attitude toward the negroes. Thousands of them long to help the negroes—if they only knew how to get about it. People at a distance imagine that it is very easy for Southern white people to help them—which only illustrates that many are not as wise as they think they are. It is easier now than it was for a dozen years after 1865. For a long time negroes did not welcome Southern co-operation—excepting always, money, Their feeling of irritated suspicion as to the Southern whites was fomented by some to the general hurt. How this was done I need not discuss now. But at this time the negroes are warming toward the Southern people. Of this there are expressions every day and every-where. Our preachers are not unwelcome now; in some quarters they are in demand.

It is a sad thing in the life of even one man when he fails to see and embrace an opportunity to do a good deed, or to forward a great movement toward the triumph of our Lord's kingdom. It is a sadder thing when a whole Church, or a whole people, misses its opportunity. We of the South have come to such a place and such a time in our history that we have again offered to us a great opportunity to help a whole race in two continents. May we be wise and faithful to make the most of it, in the love of God and of man!

It is true that our path, since the war, has been blocked in many ways. But we are not blameless; some of us have made the most of our excuses. We have accepted our dismissal too readily. We might have done more; we ought to have done more; we are going to do more. Thousands of our people will help them whenever they see the opportunity. Truth claims for our people more than they have received of recognition. After all, they have helped in many ways. There are few churches or school-houses in all the South, built for the use of the negroes since the war, in which the money of Southern white people has not been freely invested. Hardly any were built without their aid: some chiefly through their help.

This much let us understand on all sides, and, if it be true, let us act upon it: Our obligation to help the negro in his social and religious development, to help him in working out his destiny, does not grow out of his relation to "our party" or to "our Church," but out of our common relation to Christ Jesus, our elder Brother, and to God, our Father. Whether in our Church or his own, we must help him in all wise and brotherly ways to work out his problem and fulfill his mission. And this we owe to God.

Note—In that noble tribute to John Wesley, "The Wesley Memorial Volume," edited by the Rev. J. O. A. Clark, D.D., LL.D., and published by Phillips & Hunt, New York—received after this chapter was written—is an interesting and well-written article on "Wesley and the Colored Race," by Rev. L. H. Holsey, one of the Bishops of the Colored Methodist Episcopal Church of America, from which I take the following extracts. Altogether noteworthy they are. Bishop Holsey says:

> The Methodist Episcopal Church, South, impoverished by the war, and scarcely able to survive the shock she had received, was unable to keep up the work she had begun and continued for so long a time. She could barely hold the ground she had gained. During the many years she had been directing the evangelical work among the negroes she had been training a body of colored ministers who were ready to take the places of the white itinerant and local preachers. Many of these retained their connection with the Church South; many of the ablest went with other bodies of Methodists. There was now aroused a great interest in the evangelization of the colored race on the part of the Northern people. They felt that every obligation required that they should do something for the negro, and at once they began the work. They found the field already prepared and white to the harvest. Preachers, leaders, and church buildings were at hand. Culture was needed, and especially organization for self-help, for hith-

erto the colored people had been provided for by others. They must now learn to provide for themselves. The African Methodist Episcopal Church had a corps of able Bishops, and a compact organization. So had the Zion Methodists, who differed from the African Methodists in but little more than name. The Methodist Episcopal Church, rich and powerful, also came into the field. The Methodist Episcopal Church established schools and colleges and has been liberal and energetic. The other bodies have shown the same zeal.

The Methodist Episcopal Church, South, gave to the colored Church which it had set up—the Colored Methodist Episcopal Church of America—all the church buildings which it had erected for its colored members, and saw it organized for important and successful work.

The effects of Methodism upon the negro race in the South, and of the Baptists, the only other body of Christians who had ever done much for the negroes, was seen during and after the late war. The negroes rose in no insurrection. They waited the issue patiently, and when the end came, and they were free, they accepted their freedom as of God. No Christian leader among them has ever been accused of any agitation that would issue in bloodshed. They felt that God, in his providence, had said to the Christians of the South: 'Take these sons of Africa and train them for me, and in my time I will call for them.' The congregations of colored Methodists, thrown upon their own resources, have nobly met the demands, and now day-schools and Sunday-schools and churches are found all over the country.

18

THESE AFRICAN-AMERICANS AND AFRICA

What is to be the grand outcome of this most remarkable of modern race movements? Can it be supposed for a moment that the tremendous energy of these numerous and vigorous African Churches is to expend itself in these United States, and almost exclusively among these six millions of Americanized Africans and their descendants? Can any thoughtful man suppose that this mighty Amazonian current of energy—energy material, intellectual, and spiritual—is in God's wide and great plans for the world limited to the negroes in this country? or that the only relations it sustains to any channels of life outside of its own are incidental and occasional overflows?

This would amount to saying: Providence brought them to America, and maintained them here in wondrous ways, "a peculiar people," in the midst of a strange race, of variant if not antagonistic tendencies, in order that they only might be redeemed from barbarism and brought to the knowledge of the truth.

To me it is simply unthinkable that in the plans of Providence for the thousands of Africans in America the millions of Africans in Africa should have no place. To my view, nothing solves the problem of their providential coming to this country, of their providential maintenance as a race in process of civilization and Christianization, of their providential emancipation about one decade before Stanley found Livingstone—that glorious John the Baptist of African civilization—that leaves Africa out.

Here in the United States they have come to Christ, the Lord of all; here they have multiplied, as did Israel in Egypt; here they have the fairest opportunity this world can give them to grow into the fullest stature of which they are capable; and here, where they now are, the great body of them will, I do not question, remain, if not to the end of time, yet long beyond the period when all doubt of their destiny will be solved, and all controversy concerning their relation to the white race will be happily ended. Here, in a climate that suits them, in the midst of a Christian population friendly to their development under laws that protect them, under conditions the most favorable possible to them, they can grow into a strong people, "made ready" by Providence for their great duties to the uncounted millions in their mother country; here they can realize, more perfectly than anywhere else under the sun, God's plan and purpose concerning them; here they can grow to be all that they can be, and thus and then be ready to do all that they can do; here they can be taught till they can teach; here training-schools may be established, whence teachers and preachers may go forth from time to time to kindle great lights of learning and saving truth in the dark places beyond the sea; here, for holy conquests in Africa, they can gather and drill a great army of enlightened and Christianized men and women; and not teachers and preachers only, but farmers, mechanics, artisans, men in all departments competent to lead the civilization of the tribes and nations in Africa. From these shores colonies can depart from time to time, as God opens the way for the great undertaking. These colonies will follow the brave explorers who blaze out the highways for the march of that coming Christian civilization that will make of the "Dark Continent" one of the brightest and noblest lands of the earth.

What they need now is to strengthen their stakes and lengthen their cords, to get themselves ready, to gather up their energies for the greatest missionary movement that ever was undertaken in the history of the Church.

They are not ready now. God overruled slavery for most gracious ends. They learned the Gospel in slavery as they could not have learned it in their native wilds, as they could not have learned it had they been made free upon their first landing upon our shores. When emancipation—anticipating Providence, it may be—came upon them, they were not fully ready for their new trials, dangers, and responsibilities. Unless we of the South had more generally and more fully realized our providential relation to them, maybe they could never have gotten ready in slavery. But, granting whatever faults were in slavery, it is certain that their training, while in bondage, had done much for them. If their antecedents, surroundings, and resources be considered, it will be allowed that they have wrought wonders since their emancipation. Their very habit of obedience as slaves enters largely into the measure of their capacity for independent Church organization, as well as their capacity for citizenship. What could they have done with a Church, or with a ballot, or with themselves, had they been converted by cargoes and turned loose, free, upon their landing? But they are learning how to do Church work, and they are learning fast. They may lack the far-seeing sagacity of statesmanship, but they have what, perhaps, is better for the growth of a Church or a nation, the promptings of a prophetic instinct as to their duty and destiny. Moreover, let it be remembered, when we are tempted to doubt of this whole perplexed problem, that they have the guiding, though unseen, hand of God. What the Lord said of Cyrus may be said of them: "I have girded thee though thou hast not known me."

They are not, it may be, as yet fully ready to lay broadly and deeply in Africa the foundations of a great civilizing and sanctifying Church. But they are getting ready. And some of them I know have glimpses now and then of the star that is to go before them in the progress of their race to its redemption. Some of them see what men wiser in this world's knowledge may not see, for they have a simple and steadfast faith in God and his word. Some of the loftier spirits among them are already looking with longing eyes and burning hearts to the home of their fathers. They begin to hear the call of the man of Africa, "Come over and help us." They begin to realize in their inmost consciousness—it flashes on them while they sing and penetrates their deepest souls while they pray—that this divine trust is theirs, to "preach Jesus and the resurrection" to the many millions of their brethren who "dwell in the land of the shadow of death." Their hearts are stirred ofttimes with the divine quickenings; and deathless impulses of which the hopes of new nations are born. And centuries after our times, when our children's children wonder why their fathers ever quarreled or fought, the historians of Africa's redemption will bless the memory both of the North and of the South.

Will the white Christians of America, when the time comes, be ready to help? Do they now read aright "the signs of the times" of the Son of man?

The chief function of the white race in America, in its relation to the evangelization of Africa, is one of *help*. It is not ours to do this work, except as we help those whom God has so strangely called and prepared. Some white Christians are now helping, perhaps, without knowing how much; perhaps, without looking beyond the poor negroes of their own communities; perhaps, without a thought of the mighty outcome of it all in other lands, and in the years and generations to come. Every dollar consecrated to giving them the Gospel while they were slaves, and since they were made free; every sermon preached to them; every lesson taught them; every good book printed for them—all has been helping forward the salvation of a continent. And when the day of God declares all things, although it may appear that thousands of slave owners in the old days, now happily gone forever, did not realize their sacred relation to this great race movement toward the cross of our common Lord, yet will it be found that thousands did recognize and discharge, to the best of their ability, their duty to these sons of the strangers. That day will reveal the love and "compassion on souls" that inspired Capers, Andrew, Pierce, Mercer, Crawford, M'Intosh, and the thousands of nameless immortals who helped to bring nearly half a million Southern negroes to Christ Jesus, while they were yet in their house of bondage. And it will reveal thousands of godly men and women who, inheriting the burdens and responsibilities of slavery, so recognized the Christ in their servants that the King will say to them: "Inasmuch as ye have done it unto one of the least of these my brethren, ye have done it unto me."

This great preparation that is to "make straight the way of the Lord" is being helped forward every day and hour; it is helped forward every time a negro is taught a truth, or is lifted up, or in any way is placed in a better position to make a man. it is helped forward every time a negro school is established, a negro church built, a negro family toned up to better thinking and better living. In a word, every good thing that has been done, that is being done, that may yet be done for the negro here, is helping him to get ready for the moral conquest of a continent.

But when I ask, "Will the white Christians of America, when the time comes, be ready?" I do not mean this unconscious co-operation with a great movement. I mean the clear-eyed vision of a great duty and a great opportunity; I mean the conscious, deliberate recognition of that duty in our broadest, boldest plans for the future work of the Church; I mean the broad-minded, true-hearted, and courageous attempt, when the time comes, to perform that duty to the utmost of human ability.

In this work all good people in this country should heartily join; for all are debtors to the Africans in America. All Christians in this country should help them to get ready. When the day comes, and it cannot be far distant, for them to enter fully upon the work, then every Christian in the land should help them to carry it on. Some have already gone as advanced guards of the coming hosts. Some left Nashville, Tennessee, in 1880, who had been made ready in one of the great training schools of the Congregationalists. And a few have gone from other Churches. There are a few white men and women at work in different parts of Africa; they have gone before. In Sierra Leone, in Senegambia, in the Ashantee Country, on the Lower Coast, the Coast Country near the Cape, in Liberia, and among the tribes nearest the British dependencies, are mission stations where the true light shines. Thousands have already come to the light and have rejoiced in it. The work that has been done is one of glorious preparation. But the missionary movement that is to save the continent must flow out of the African Churches in the United States. "A tidal wave of blessing," to use the words of Bishop Holsey, one of their own race, "must sweep back upon the shores of Africa."

When the colored Baptists in the United States send missionaries to Africa, then let the entire Baptist power of America stand back of them and help and nourish them as there may be need. When the Congregationalist negroes send missionaries, let the entire Congregationalist power help them in all their work. When the Methodist negroes begin to send out missionaries in good earnest, when they begin to organize "Mission conferences" in Africa, then in, this work, if never before, or after, or elsewise, let the entire power of American Methodism unite to forward their great design. The Methodist Episcopal Church, South, has in her organization now few names of the negro race, but she has children in every colored Church in America, and they call to her to help them; and this Church will hear the cry of her children, and she will help them.

In such a work as this at least all Methodism, I say not American Methodism only, should unite as one body and one soul. But the call is pre-eminently to American Methodism and peculiarly to American Episcopal Methodism. This pre-eminent and special call grows out of the relations these Methodisms sustain to each other and to the negroes; also out of the opportunity God gives them, as indicated and measured by the greatness of their numbers and their power. If once our brother in black was the innocent "occasion" of an unfraternal parting, may it not, in the good providence of God, be some day his high office to unite us again, at least in all the love and sympathy of a genuine and deathless brotherhood of mutual help and genuine co-operation?

Do we not owe this debt to Africa? Her sons helped mightily to clear the forests before the march of our population. Their toils have added untold millions to the wealth of our country. Their hands have helped to build up great cities and great highways in all our States. They, at least, are not to blame for the horrors and exasperations of our fratricidal war. They deserve everlasting honor for their heroic patience and Christian waiting during that fiery trial of their faith. Modern times have not given to the world a sublimer expression of a steadfast faith in the all-wise providence of God.

When God's time comes, and surely we are nearing the hour when the day will break upon them and us, let us be found among them who know the "day of the Lord." We may be sure of it, *God's hand is upon this people.* When he speaks to them "that they move forward," as he did to Israel on the shores of the Red Sea, let us be sure that the "pillar of cloud and of fire" will go before them, and that the "Captain of the Lord's host" will lead them on.

When the children of Israel went out of Egypt, under the "high hand" and the "outstretched arm" of the God of their fathers, they "spoiled the Egyptians," for their heathen oppressors were hard of heart and would not do them justice, nor "let Israel go," nor forward them on their journey. But *we are not of Egypt; we are Christ's, the Lord's.* We must and we will, in gratitude to God and to these our brothers, in the love of humanity and in the love of Christ, send them away on their divine mission with "blessings" and with "gifts."

Is there a more inspiring thought in connection with the future of the Christian religion? Millions of Christianized negroes in America sending and carrying the Gospel, that alone brings life and immortality to light, to uncounted millions in their native Africa, while millions of Christians of the white race join hands and hearts in helping on the glorious work. There never existed in the circumstances and relations of two races such an opportunity of doing missionary work on a continent-wide scale. Would God there were some Christian Moses or Paul to lead the triumphant march! There never was a work for God and man in which the good angels would more gladly join.

O, Thou Christ of God! Thou "mightiest among the holy and holiest among the mighty!" Thou who didst take upon thyself "the form of a servant" that Thou mightest make all men free, give to us the "fullness of Thy spirit," that we, Thy unworthy disciples, may have wisdom and grace and courage to make ready for the duties of the morrow by faithfully performing all our duty of to-day, toward these our brethren, who came unwillingly to our guardian-ship long before our fathers were born; whom Thou hast kept as "a peculiar people" in our midst, and hast blessed beyond any people who were ever enslaved; whom Thou hast made free by many and strange providences, and to whom Thou hast given a message of hope and salvation for multiplied millions of their kindred who wait for Thy coming as "those who watch for the morning!"

19

SENATOR EUSTIS ON THE NEGRO PROBLEM

(New York *Independent*, November 8, 1888)

I confess to a degree of interest bordering upon impatience when the papers announced that Senator Eustis would present his views upon the Negro problem in the October *Forum*. Having twice read the Senator's article my interest is not abated; it is rather increased, not by what is in the article, but by what is not in it. The article is a very short one for such a subject, discussed by a United States Senator; perhaps half of it, instead of giving us light upon a very difficult subject, gives us very commonplace satires upon the inconsistencies of the New England friends of the Negro. While reading these bits of satire my feeling was—have heard that so long and so often and from so many—"rats!" A review of the Senator's article in a Northern paper that came to me yesterday, with a good deal about the "slave-driver's whip," I put in the same category—"chestnuts!" This sort of thing is as stale as it is unprofitable.

No doubt the New England people are inconsistent; most people are—especially earnest people. No doubt a good deal that the Senator says of the New England practice in dealing with the actual Negro in Massachusetts and the New England doctrine as to the ideal Negro in Louisiana is just enough; but it is not a discussion of the Negro question in the United States.

I say in the United States, for no misconception is more complete or fatal than that which makes the Negro question a mere "home-rule" (one of the Senator's expressions), local, municipal incident. Most of the Negroes are in the South, to be sure; but what they are, what they are to be, concerns every citizen in Maine and California as surely as in Georgia or Texas. Certainly the Negro question is more insistent and exigent in the Southern States, but it vitally concerns this whole Nation. I write the word so, for we are now a nation, and not a mere partnership ("limited") of States—we will not write it state, they are not mere "taxing districts."

The American people in Chicago feel more keenly than American people in Georgia the troubles that grow out of the dangerous presence in that great city of more than half a million foreigners, many thousands of them bitterly antagonistic to the essential facts and spirit of our civilization. (Since beginning this article I have read in a paper that the Chicago anarchists have organized Sunday-schools to teach their children their diabolisms!) But what these foreigners may now be, what they may become, what they may do, is not a mere " home-rule," Chicago, 111., or North-western question; it is also an Atlanta, a Georgia, a Southern, above all a national, question. If for no other reason—and may be this is least important—these foreigners in Chicago may some day hold the balance of power in an election that would give to Louisiana a very unsatisfactory President.

If there has been any fanaticism, intolerance, or spirit of intermeddling mixed up in the efforts that have been made by Northern people to improve the Negro's character as well as condition, to educate and fit him for American citizenship, such infirmities may deserve rebuke; but if Senator Eustis thinks that any American citizen is out of his place in seeking to make the Negro a fit citizen, he so totally misconceives the whole question that it is impossible for him to reason justly or profitably upon it. His point of view makes the understanding of the problem to him a simple impossibility. It cannot be doubted that the Senator did his best in his contribution to the *Forum;* with his view and the light he has, one could hardly do better.

It would have been unjust to the Senator to have expected in his

article commendations of the great efforts that have been made—
with vast outlay of money and noble lives—to educate the Negro
into Christian citizenship. The history of this great movement is
evidently unknown to him; he might have learned a great deal
from the important schools in New Orleans—Leland, Straight,
the Methodist University named for the city—to say nothing of
the University for Negro youths that Louisiana gives $10,000 a
year to; and Godman, in Gilbert Seminary at Baldwin, on the La
Teche, might have given him most valuable information. Perhaps
he deserves censure for not improving his fine opportunities to
study the Negro problem in its most important aspects.

But granting all that is justly due to his lack of information on
these vital issues, I must confess to surprise in reading such words
as these:

> We insist that it is time for the Northern people to acknowledge
> that inasmuch as this race question directly affects the interests,
> the civilization, and the destiny of the Southern people, to them
> alone should be confided the task and the responsibility of solving
> it. To them it is a domestic and a home-rule question surpassing
> in its importance and gravity every national question. The South-
> ern people never concern themselves about matters which are of
> purely municipal cognizance in the North. Their political educa-
> tion has taught them to respect the propriety of State comity.

If there were seven millions of Chinese in New England, citizens and voters, and as unqualified for citizenship as are the majority of the Negroes in the South, this would not be a state of
things, in even Senator Eustis's view, of "purely municipal cognizance." In such a case, the South being as rich as New England
and New England as poor as the South is, wise and good Southerners would not be hindered by any "proprieties of State comity"
from helping to educate these seven millions of Chinamen into
something like fitness for citizenship. In such a case would Boston
receive the missionaries of education kindly? Not if the supposed
Chinese had been slaves for more than a century; that is, not at the
first. After a time they would be received kindly, as after a time
teachers of Negro youth in Louisiana will be received kindly.

Undoubtedly all who understand the subject will agree with Senator Eustis as to the surpassing importance of this question to the Southern people; it dwarfs all others. There is no diversity of opinion among us on this point. The right adjustment of the Negro citizen to our institutions is vital to us; in the long run vital to the nation.

For this very reason I protest against the doctrine that the South is to be left alone to deal with this problem—too great for the whole people.

The facts leading up to the present conditions of life in the South—the bringing of the Negroes to this country, slavery and all its belongings, the War (which, whether one party calls it "the Rebellion," or the other calls it " the Confederate Movement," was most truly a Revolution, wide-spread, radical, and final as to what went before it), emancipation, enfranchisement and its consequents, all these are facts, not of Southern history only, but of American history. The Negro problem is no more a matter of "purely municipal cognizance" in the South than was the Revolution whose history tells of Fort Sumter and Appomatox, and all between. It is as impossible to apportion responsibilities for the past as it is to limit the obligations of the present time to a particular section—looking after matters of "purely municipal cognizance."

If the Northern people were minded to leave the South to work out this problem unaided they would be guilty of an immeasurable injustice, not to the Negro alone, but to every Southern white man, woman and child—born and to be born—as well; would be guilty of an unpardonable sin against the whole American nation, to say nothing of that which is supreme—the Kingdom of Jesus Christ in the earth. For, whoever brought the Negroes to this country, whoever held them in slavery for shorter or longer times, the Northern people, under God, made them free people and voters, and so made the Negro problem a matter of concern to the whole American people. The North would be forever disgraced if her people for any reason—"the proprieties of State comity," or any other—abandoned to ignorance the poor people they burdened with the contentions and responsibilities of citizenship.

While slavery endured there was for the Southern people—the white and the black people—a *modus vivendi,* though the Negroes were ignorant. But slavery gone forever, the Negroes not only free but voters, and permanently ignorant and degraded through ignorance and the moral evils inevitable to ignorance, there is no possible *modus vivendi* in the long run of history. For the moment, and for argument's sake, admitting that secession was as wicked as the most devoted and fierce Unionist ever believed it to be—that we of the South deserved very great punishment for our unhappy relation to slavery and our devotion to the Confederacy—certainly no man since Nero's time is cruel enough to believe that the Southern white people deserve the punishment that would befall them if one third of their population were forever condemned to citizenship—and ignorance. In such a case we would cry out with Cain, branded and banished, " My punishment is greater than I can bear."

It may be answered, the supposition does not fit the case. Then I affirm that it does. For we of the Southern white race, since 1865, have been too poor to educate the Negro into true citizenship; we have not been able rightly to educate our own children. More; had we been able, we were not at the close of the War, and few of us are to-day (October, 1888), disposed to do much, if any thing, for the education of the Negro outside of the work done in the common schools. It is but simple truth to say most of us have had little faith even in this common-school education of Negro children; perhaps I should have written, little love for it. Some few Southern people may take offense at this statement. It is absurd to do so; every man of us knows it to be true.

Outside of the common schools we of the South have not done enough—or even thought seriously of doing enough—to furnish one tenth of these schools with teachers of their own race. And now, and for a long time to come, there must be in the South Negro teachers for Negro common schools, or there will be no schools, or so few that there will not be enough to count in the census. But there are now in the South fully sixteen thousand common schools for Negro children; they are uniformly taught by Negro teachers. All of them that are worth the small salaries they receive were educated in the higher schools carried on by Northern money and Northern men and women.

The exceptions to the foregoing statement are few. 1. In most of the Southern States are institutions for training Negro teachers aided by the State Governments. Nearly all the teachers are Northern people, or Negroes trained in schools founded and taught by Northern people. There are some bright and notable exceptions. For example, in Claflin University, Orangeburg, S. C.— number of students, 1887-88, 700; adding preparatory school students, 925—are three South Carolina men, good and true, also Democrats, teaching in perfect harmony with Dr. Dunton and his Northern corps of instructors. In broad contrast with the views of Senator Eustis is the statesmanship of Governor Richardson, who recommended the act of the Legislature at Columbia last winter that placed an extra $5,000 at Claflin for its general betterment, and the intelligent and constant interest in the University of General James Izlar, of Orangeburg, one of the "Confederate brigadiers," also "Chairman of the Executive Committee of the Democratic Party in his State." Governor Richardson made them an admirable speech at their Commencement last May. Governor Seay, of Alabama, is like him on this subject; studies the facts, and is doing all he can to promote the cause of education among his Negro fellow-citizens. Senator Colquitt, of Georgia, is the steady friend of this cause. There are a few others like them; "may their tribe increase!" 2. Some of the Southern white Churches are beginning to stir in this duty. They have not as yet done much compared with the Northern Churches, but they have begun, and they will never draw back. This movement is in the Christian conscience of the Southern Church. It has been hindered and well-nigh strangled; but the day of deliverance comes; they will go steadily on. It must be so while men and women believe in Jesus Christ and care for the human race.

The "supposition does fit the case." Suppose the contributions in money and personal service made by the Northern people toward the solution of this problem had not been made. Who can suppose that our case, bad as it is, would not have been inconceivably worse? Nearly eight years ago I said in a little book that if Northern people had not done this work, if nobody had done it, the South would have been uninhabitable. Reflection, observation over the entire South, special study of this question, with uncommon opportunities for getting at its facts, confirm the opinion reached long ago.

If any shall answer me, "If Northern people had only kept their hands off, Southern people would have done this work," I must reply, and sorrowfully enough, "You will have extraordinary difficulty in giving reasons for your belief." Knowing well what Southern white people have done and have not done—knowing better than Northern people do the attitude of thought and feeling we have held toward those who have been engaged in the work of educating the Negroes, I must confess I do not know any good reason for supposing that we of the Southern white race would have carried on these great training-schools if Northern people had left us alone with our " home-rule" issues and matters of " purely municipal cognizance."

The South has done a vast work in educating the Negroes; a work as little understood, as I chance to know, by many Northern people—and some of them quite as prominent as Senator Eustis—as the work of the great training-schools is unknown to most Southern people. More than fifty million dollars, all told, has been expended upon the education of the Negroes since 1865. More than half of this has been paid by the South in the support of the sixteen thousand public schools for Negro youth—these cost much more than all the colleges. Every year increases the disproportion. In every Southern State will be expended during the school year 1888-89 a much larger sum upon the Negro common schools than all outside contributions to education in these States. The Southern whites pay most of the taxes. If, for example, Georgia be worth four hundred millions, the taxable property of the Negroes is not more than ten millions.[1] It is idle to argue about

---

[1] After this article was written I undertook a very thorough investigation of the subject,

the motives of Southern people in dividing the public-school money without distinction of race (though it is uncharity to assign other than a good motive), for the free school was inevitable in the logic of events after the War, and free schools for both races were inevitable, if there were free schools for either.

It is as singular as it is suggestive that a man in Senator Eustis's position, writing on so important a subject—a subject so many-sided and so far-reaching in every direction—should, in his contribution to the solution of the Negro problem, have taken no account of the history of the education of these people since 1865. If he did not think of it at all it is very surprising; if he did think of it his silence is amazing. Nearly one million of these people are at school in the South, and about two millions of them can read. Such facts and what they signify are worth the consideration of even Senator Eustis. Whether the Negro's education be for good or evil, it enters vitally into the discussion of his case before the American people. Leaving out of his argument so essential a part of the subject-matter, it is not surprising that the Senator assumes so pessimistic a position as the title of his article indicates—a view that, of all people, we of the South should be slow to adopt.

He writes, for the most part, of a "Race Antagonism" that he believes to be invincible in its sentiments—if one does not wish to say prejudices—on both sides. This antagonism he tells us grows out of race differences inherent and insuperable; but when seeking an illustration for the smiting of Boston inconsistency he so far forgets his stilted philosophy as to write after this fashion:

> One who had only superficially studied the agitation of the Negro question in Massachusetts might be led to believe that there was no prejudice against him in that State. He might expect to find that the Negro is there treated like any other member of so-

---

obtaining the facts from the highest official sources for use in the preparation of an article for *Harper's Magazine* for June, 1889. The entire sum expended by Virginia, North Carolina, South Carolina, Georgia. Florida, Alabama, Mississippi, Louisiana, Texas, Arkansas, Tennessee, and Kentucky, since 1868, upon Negro education is more than $37,000,000. In 1888 these States expended $10,926,000 upon public education; of this sum $5,165,000 went for Negro education: about $3,100,000 to common schools for Negro children, the rest to Normal schools for the training of their teachers.   A.G.H.

ciety; free to indulge in social intercourse; free to intermarry, and free to associate in private and public with white people. If there is equality between the two races these suggestions should not shock society in Massachusetts. The people of France have never offensively advertised their sympathy with the Negro, and have never lectured other nations about their unfair and unjust treatment of him. Yet even on the question of intermarriage, white society there has never discriminated against the Negro. If he be a gentleman, the Negro from the French islands of the West Indies If as always been received in the fashionable *salons* of the Faubourg St. Germain in Paris, where dwell the descendants of the ancient noblesse of France, a circle certainly as exclusive and as aristocratic as any society in Boston. This Negro from the French West Indies, thus socially entertained, is the same kind of Negro that we have in this country, for they were both piously transported by Boston shipowners from the same country in Africa.

This row of posts is badly out of line; it is not my business to straighten it for him. He tells us this race antagonism grows out of conscious superiority on the part of the white man and conscious inferiority on the part of the Negro—a consciousness not changeable by any amount of culture in the Negro; he tells us that French *salons* in the Faubourg St. Germain, most exclusive of fashionable and aristocratic circles, make no bones of receiving a West India Negro if a gentleman; he tells us that the West Indian is the same kind of Negro we have in the South.

The Senator will excuse people who do not follow implicitly a leader who can in so short an article commit himself, and in apparent unconsciousness, to propositions so utterly antagonistic and destructive of each other. It is probable that the Senator, following the drift of old-time views, wrote hastily. The social question I do not now, or at any time, argue about; it is more than useless. It will adjust itself or else never be adjusted. But this is very clear to me: if the white man be so superior as Senator Eustis thinks he has no reason to be afraid for his position.

The most significant thing in Senator Eustis's article is what it lacks; there is no place in his philosophy of the subject for the Providence of God, except in the assumption that God in the beginning fixed upon the subject difficulties that have been, that are, that ever will be insuperable as to any adjustment or outcome of a sort the friends of education and religion hope for. Perhaps such questions are outside the Senator's meditations. I do not know; the doubt is raised in justice to him.

But this is certain to all who do believe in God's providence in this as in all the affairs of men: no view of the Negro problem that leaves God out—that leaves out the conservative and saving influences of the Christian religion—can add any thing of value to the discussion.

The facts do not warrant the Senator's despondent view. If, as he intimates, the Negroes of the South have had more help than ever came to any other people, I answer: This is true; and no people ever made a better use of the help that was given them. Their progress in twenty years is marvelous; there is no chapter in the history of education like that which tells this story.

But it is encouraging that Senator Eustis wrote his article. It is a good sign. Southern people are thinking about this subject more than heretofore. The Senator no doubt did his best; his effort may induce other men in his circle to ask concerning the facts. When they find out what the facts are they can write so as to make a contribution of value to the discussion. And his example is valuable; it helps break the *taboo*.

Whatever political theory men form or oppose; whatever their speculative opinions about the origin of races; whatever their notions concerning color or caste; whatever their relations heretofore to slavery and what went along with it, this is absolutely certain: no question involving the rights and wrongs of men, civilized or savage, white or black, was ever yet settled so that it would stay settled by any system of mere repression. And to those who believe in Jesus Christ it is equally certain that nothing can be rightly settled that is not settled in harmony with the teachings of the Sermon on the Mount. If there be a Divine Providence no good man need be afraid to do right to-day; nay, he will fear only doing wrong.

ATTICUS G. HAYGOOD
Decatur, Ga.

20

Is It Education or Suppression?

(An article by Senator Eustis, of Louisiana, in *The Forum*, on the Negro Problem, was replied to, in our issue of November 8, by Dr. Haygood, who could not allow so bitter an expression against the colored race to go unrebuked. We have asked a number of prominent educators in the South, and others in the South, who we knew were intelligently interested in the subject, to give their opinion of Dr. Haygood's views and of the Negro question. These men are all of Southern origin, and we suppose all or nearly all are Democrats. Only Mr. Cable now lives in the North.—ED. INDEPENDENT.)

BY PROFESSOR WILLIAM F. BASKERVIL,
Vanderbilt University, Nashville, Tenn.

To THE EDITOR OF THE INDEPENDENT: With many Southerners the views expressed by Senator Eustis in *The Forum* for October are undoubtedly popular. But their number is yearly growing less. Those who believe with the Senator almost invariably pursue his plan of attack. Articles of this kind, in which it is openly alleged or skillfully insinuated that the friends of the Negro are striving after social equality, might bring about race antagonism if there were not still among us a leaven of common sense and of religion. Common sense says, with Dr. Haygood, "The social question I do not now, or at any time, argue about; it is more than useless. It will adjust itself or else never be adjusted." Religion, too, joins her voice to his in saying, "If there be a Divine Providence no good man need be afraid to do right to-day; nay, he will fear only doing wrong."

I am glad Dr. Haygood answered the Senator's article. He knows the Southern people and the Negro problem better than any other man in the South. Our respect and esteem he has always had. His bold and fearless attitude has commanded our admiration. His wise and steady course along this straight and narrow way has won our confidence and our trust. We now perceive that he is as wise as he is fearless. At first he met with what seemed to be general censure. But a far-seeing man, on being asked what would be the effect of this outcry against Dr. Haygood, said then, "It will only serve to make good and thoughtful men rally to him."

Giving the Negro the ballot—that dangerous weapon in the hands of the ignorant and the degraded—was one of the wisest blunders ever committed. As a political move it was a complete blunder. Reconstruction times first—then Democratic ascendency. No wonder it made Republican *politicians* sick. But in the hands of Providence it will yet prove to have been consummate wisdom. It has placed a heavy burden upon us, it is true, the heaviest a civilized people ever yet has had to bear, but not too heavy for the American people. Now the whole nation is interested in preparing—nay, is compelled to prepare—the Negro for the proper use and appreciation of citizenship. Only two factors really enter into this problem: religion and education. How best to promote the one and in what way to provide for the other are matters of supreme importance to every Christian patriot.

BY GEORGE W. CABLE,
Northampton, Mass.

EDITOR OF THE INDEPENDENT: I have already discussed Senator Eustis's paper in *The Forum* of last December. I do not think any utterance of mine varies in principle from any made by Dr. Hay-good in his criticism. Yet I gladly accept the invitation to comment on Dr. Haygood's paper. I give my heartiest applause to his main statement, that it is folly for the South and shame for the North to call the Negro question less than national.

He seems to me quite as clearly right when he welcomes writers of Senator Eustis's kind into the arena of literary debate. I count it an incalculable misfortune that for twenty years the nation has left the discussion of this great question almost totally to the floors of Congress, where in the nature of the case it is bound to suffer fatally from heat, and to the columns of the daily press, where it is as inevitably bound to suffer fatally from haste. The difficulties of the problem demand that it be subjected to the most careful, dispassionate, studious discussion; a discussion purged of personalities, partisan rallying cries, and unauthenticated conjectures and recriminations, especially a *progressive* discussion, where each particular division of the question once settled—once fairly taken prisoner and paroled, so to speak—shall not have to be fought over again. Such discussion it is reasonable to hope for only, or at least mainly, through the medium of the nation's more distinctively literary utterance, as it comes to us in the dispassionate columns of our magazines, reviews, and periodicals not devoted primarily to news.

It may be said in reply that that is all very well for educated people, people of studious tastes. But, in fact, it is just the educated people that have first got to settle this great question. That done there is no other question on our continent that will be so nearly settled altogether.

Let us rejoice in the New South of material development, and even read in our daily newspapers statistics without signature or official sanction and often palpably padded; but neither official nor conjectural figures can tell the value it will be to the South and the nation, to bring into the clear light and air of a calm, friendly, and faithful national literary debate *the principles* of law and order upon which a New South must be founded if it is to endure.

BY PROFESSOR CHARLES FOSTER SMITH,
Vanderbilt University, Nashville, Tenn.

As to Senator Eustis's article, I think it is just about as good and as bad as Senator Chandler's" Our Southern Masters," and perhaps the best thing that could be done with both would be to print them together in one pamphlet and send them out to neutralize each other. I indorse the spirit and the matter of Dr. Haygood's reply to Senator Eustis's article. Dr. Haygood is the one Southern man whom I should be willing to follow blindfold on the Negro question. He understands the subject. What his heart prompts and his head approves he has the courage to do—always the right, as he sees it, in this, as in all other matters.

The whole philosophy of the question and the germ of all rules for its treatment lie, it seems to me, in Dr. Haygood's last paragraph:

> Whatever political theory men form or oppose; whatever their speculative opinions about the origin of races; whatever their notions concerning color or caste; whatever their relations heretofore to slavery and what went along with it, this is absolutely certain: no question involving the rights and wrongs of men, civilized or savage, white or black, was ever yet settled so that it would stay settled by any system of mere repression. And to those who believe in Christ it is equally certain that nothing can be rightly settled that is not settled in harmony with the Sermon on the Mount. If there be a Divine Providence no good man need be afraid to do right to-day; nay, he will fear only doing wrong.

The conscience of the country, North and South, needs to be quickened just here—that the whites must do right toward the Negro and grant him all that the law allows. And it will do no good to frighten our people with suggestions as to what may come of doing right, the bugbear of social equality, and all such. To all such suggestions there is one sufficient reply, "I am not responsible for the result; I am only responsible for doing right."

The great trouble is that people are apt to assume that the Negroes cannot be educated, cannot be trained into good, intelligent, property-holding citizens, then to seek the facts to support the assumption. And, as facts of all kinds are always lying about loose, a man can generally find the facts he is after, especially if he is looking for that kind and no other. Moreover, most men begin with emancipation and seek back for four thousand years, whereas nearly all the important facts lie this side of 1865.

All hope of the solution of the Negro question lies in the hypothesis that it can be worked out by the same agencies that would be applied in the case of any other race. A study of the facts on this hypothesis brings me increasing encouragement from year to year. Education and property are good for the white man, and, as a Tennessee mountaineer said to me last summer, "What is good for the white man must be good for the nigger." To stimulate and help the Negro to get an education, to encourage and secure him in the possession of property, to grant him all that the law allows, is the least and the best that the white race can do. As to education, he has shown an eagerness, a persistency, a success which do him infinite credit; in point of property his record is not so good, yet, in places where he has had a chance, he has done surprisingly well.

It is not worth while to suppose that any of the Southern States would submit again to such governments as those of the "carpet-bag" *regime.* But happily that danger is past in most of them, and I am far from believing that suppression of the colored vote is the only way to prevent anywhere a return of the horrors of the " carpet-bag" *regime.* Many of us can now see that Governor Chamberlain meant to try honestly the experiment whether honest government were possible in a State with a Negro majority without suppression of the votes of any class. Whether he could have succeeded then it is now impossible to say.

At all events, I believe in discussion of the question. If there is a right and wrong in the matter men's consciences must be quickened by discussion. It is still as true as when Pericles said it, "The great impediment to action is, not discussion, but the want of that knowledge which is gained by discussion preparatory to action."

BY PROFESSOR ROBERT T. HILL,

University of Texas, Austin

To THE EDITOR OF THE INDEPENDENT: Dr. Haygood's reply to Senator Eustis embodies, in my opinion, the only logical conclusion which can be reached by any serious citizen of our nation who has rubbed against the Negro question, be he from the North or the South.

Senator Eustis's article was not only an attempt to clog the progress of the only solution of the problem—education, technical and moral—but also a dangerous torch which may have been influential in inciting the present reaction upon the part of certain of my misguided fellow-countrymen against the Negro as seen at Wahalak.

The young white men and women in the South are the real sufferers from the race prejudices so boldly championed by Senator Eustis; for so poisonous is this evil of continual nursing of an obsolete civil position which we must sooner or later abandon that it seems to me immoral that our young Southerners should be forced out of contact and sympathy with all the grand scientific, economic, and social impulses that have made the quarter of a century since Appomatox most truly great.

There is but one solution to the Negro problem—he must be helped and educated into intelligent citizenship. Lack of Christian sympathy and the toleration and instigation of opposition to this end are the most cruel indictment that can be made against us, and one for which there is no apology except that Dr. Haygood's leaven is surely working.

The time has not arrived anywhere for miscellaneous social mixture, and a mingling of the two races in public schools in the South would be inexpedient; but if helping, protecting, educating, and elevating the Negro out of savagery be a crime, what is humanity?

The Southern people, who give millions to Christianize foreign people, must take the Negro by the hand of sympathy as well as form and help him from the degradation into which, if left to himself, he will fall deeper and deeper. Our apathy ill becomes our professions, and, viewed from any standpoint, will dwarf and retard our progress in every direction.

BY PROFESSOR F. C. WOODWARD,
University of South Carolina

To the Editor of the Independent: Dr. Haygood in all his utterances on the "Negro question" holds the vantage-ground of an unprejudiced thinker. This cannot be said of most deliverances on this subject; the discussion seems to have fallen, ordinarily, to men too interested or too biased to see any other than their own side, and has had less the appearance of an effort to reach light on the issue than of a hot political tilt in the arena of dialectics. Half the difficulties hampering the situation are the result of the well-written articles and eloquent speeches with which every sore spot on the question has been unremittingly rubbed to acute rawness.

There has been too much confidence in patent remedies—an unreasonable expectation of a quick settlement of the question. It was hopeless to expect that either black or white could, in two or three decades, solve the sphinx riddles of the war and fit themselves readily to a radically changed order of things. In normal and favorable conditions the wished-for equality of civil and political rights should hardly have been looked for under a half century or more. Were it not for the heat of war still quickening all pulses, still unsettling judgments, still putting sentiment for common sense and prejudice for sound policy, all would regard the present state of the case as a satisfactory advance toward settlement. The trouble is that we are still applying war methods to the development of peace measures. The vanity of this attempt is seen in the fact that these measures are growths, and not manufactures. Not all the compulsion of science can hurry an oak-bud to maturity; a hapless turn of the foot may crush it.

It is noteworthy that nearly all agree to let the social evolution of this matter alone, and that, since the decision of the Supreme Court on the civil-rights bill, most disputants have consented, apparently, to leave the adjustment of these matters also to time and education and like agencies. No one, however, seems to think of applying these striking analogies to the settlement of the Negro's political status—the one phase of the general question still under treatment. Why should controversy and denunciation be expected to help the colored man to an intelligent exercise of the franchise and not to the enjoyment of social and public privileges? Why may not time and education and experience be relied on to bring about the adjustment of his political relations? If any phase of this question is liable to natural and peaceable methods, this, more than any, demands the application of such methods.

This is no appeal for *laissez-faire*, but for reasonable and judicious treatment of an acute disorder. The South could not, if she would, smother this issue. She would not! No one need doubt her anxiety to settle it for the good of all concerned. She has brushed the tears and blood of the four years' agony and the grime and sweat of the succeeding struggle from her eyes, and has fixed them intently on the problem she must solve; let faith and hope and love stand by and encourage, and all will be well.

Even from Southern lips the cry is not unfrequently heard, "O that this too, too solid South would melt!" But heretofore the chill blasts of the north wind have forced the South to draw her mantle about her for protection; she would gladly welcome the warm, cheering beams of a new rising sun!

BY W. M. BECKNER,
Editor of "The Winchester Democrat" Winchester, Ky.

To the Editor of the Independent: The Negro population of Kentucky is of a better class than that of the Cotton States; but even here it presents problems not easy of solution. That these will be worked out, however, none who believes in God and in the adjusting influences of American institutions can for a moment doubt. The circle of those who recognize the "Brother in Black" as a useful element in the social forces of the South is widening from year to year. It is idle to talk about sending him away. He docs not want to go, and we could not afford to give him up. Even if it were desirable to get rid of him, where is the power to effect his removal?

His mission on this continent may be inferior in scope, but it is no less manifest than that of the Caucasian. He has a record of moral and intellectual improvement without a parallel in the history of the world, but I am not one of those who fear that he may outstrip the Anglo-Saxon in the race of life.

In Kentucky there has been a steady progress in public sentiment with reference to the Negro. Before the war he was a chattel, and held a place just a little above that of the race-horse or the blooded cow. Then came emancipation, and his former owners for a while felt a resentment toward those who had so violently deprived them of their property, which in part spent its force on the freed-man himself.

The first movement on the part of the State toward recognizing him as an element in society was the proposition to allow him to testify in the courts. Just and reasonable as it now appears, it was at first received with a storm of disapproval, and seemed for a time to have destroyed the prospects for political preferment of all who openly favored it. But sentiment has changed entirely, and the first and most conspicuous advocate of this step is to-day a popular member of Congress, having been three times elected without serious opposition in a district composed of what was once the strongest stock-holding counties in the State. Then came the question of manhood suffrage, which was accepted, under the pressure of the Constitutional Amendment, with an ill-grace indeed. Views have changed, however, until all thoughtful men see that our fellow-citizens of African descent give the South twenty additional votes in Congress, and are willing to concede that, considering their condition and environments, they have used the right to vote in a manner creditable and encouraging. Then came the agitation with reference to their riding on the cars; but this no longer disturbs the public mind, and has become a question of condition and not of race. Colored people are now found in railway coaches of every class, and nobody notices their presence if decent in appearance and orderly in conduct.

The evolution of a system for the education of the Negro has been an interesting feature of our State economy. It took several years to bring us to the point of giving him for this purpose the taxes that he paid. This was at the time considered by our people quite liberal and magnanimous. It soon became apparent, however, that it fell far short of our obligation to a class of our population so helpless and needy, and now with universal approval the law gives to the Negro child for school purposes the same *pro rata* that is enjoyed by the offspring of those who pay the bulk of the taxes. I would not be understood as claiming that prejudice in Kentucky has died out in a single generation; but I do assert that the Negro has a position here very different from that which he held at the close of the war. Time and intelligence have wrought wonders, and he is no longer engaged in working out his destiny "with fear and trembling," but is recognized as having fixed rights which none care to deny him. He is acquiring property, establishing family names, realizing the importance of social standing, and learning the value of intelligence. There is still a race antagonism in Kentucky to the extent that social equality is neither allowed nor desired, and that schools, in view of the best interests of all, are and must be kept separate. Intermarriage between the races is forbidden bylaw, and would not be tolerated by the thoughtful elements, either white or black. The masses of the colored people are still so far behind in educational advantages that they cannot find congenial associations save among themselves. The middle wall of partition has not been broken down, but it is no longer maintained in a spirit of rancor or bitterness. It is simply a necessity of the situation, and is acquiesced in by the Negroes themselves without question or complaint. Whoever attempts to predict what will be done in the future with reference to the Negro question is apt to utter nonsense, just as our fathers have done before us.

My own opinion has been for some years past that education will relieve the South of the most serious evils connected with the Negro problem. An ignorant man is not apt to change his location, because he prefers to bear the ills he has rather than "fly to others that he knows not of." Those who have observed must have seen that intelligent colored people emigrate, as do the whites, and seek such places as offer the best facilities for earning a livelihood in their chosen spheres of service. As their condition is improved the dense Negro population of the South will be scattered and the race will find itself a factor in the further development of every section of the Union. With more general intelligence will come a better observance of the moral code and a higher conception of the responsibilities of life. Of course there must be a decided feeling of antagonism toward the Negro on the part of the white people of Louisiana, or else a politician like Senator Eustis would not have written such a paper as he contributed to the October number of *The Forum;* but even its tone is different from what it would have been twenty years ago. It shows that the distinguished writer is not without appreciation of the better qualities of the " man and brother," but cannot tear himself away from the prejudices of "a day that is dead" and discuss dispassionately questions which time and the good sense of the people, under God, are settling to the glory of a country great enough to furnish equal rights before the law to all races of men. I have spent my entire life in the South, and belong to the dominant political party of that section. I have among the Negroes many warm friends whom I esteem, and who, in my intercourse with them, have shown that they possess some of the noblest attributes of manhood.

God knows I do not feel toward them any sentiment of race antagonism; neither do they expect from me more than they are entitled to in view of their culture and condition. Does not the course of events in Kentucky give reasonable ground to hope that the day is not far distant when, throughout the Republic, it will be realized in heart and expressed in act, by white and black alike,

That one sure link doth all control

To one close brotherhood,

For who the race of men doth love

Loves also Him above?

BY JOHN H. BOYD,

Durant, Miss.

To the Editor of the Independent: There are many points worthy of notice in Dr. Haygood's admirable reply to Senator Eustis's article on "Race Antagonism"; but I shall comment only on what is said about the Negro question being one of national concern. It seems self-evident that now, since the Negro has been enfranchised, he ought to be fitted to vote intelligently and from principle, that the condition of seven million citizens must be of interest to all parts of a common country, and that the South in her present state is not equal to the task of fitting the Negro for the duties of citizenship. If these are not self-evident truths Dr. Haygood has set them forth so clearly and forcibly that they have all the weight and authority of intuition.

Even if national welfare were not jeopardized by the present condition of the Negro, philanthropy alone should seek to raise him to a higher plane. "No American citizen is out of place in seeking to make the Negro a fit citizen." There can be no officious intermeddling in this matter. May Slaters and Hands be multiplied! May more Fisk and Claflin Universities be founded! May more Northern teachers come to elevate these poor black children into Christian manliness! There is, however, another spirit of "intermeddling." Let me make a move with Dr. Haygood's own pieces:

If there were seven millions of Chinese in New England as unqualified for citizenship as are the majority of the Negroes in the South; "if by Southern legislation they were made citizens and voters, and by their votes should place corrupt men in power, squander the State's revenues, levy oppressive taxation on lands owned entirely by the native whites; if the good people of New England should overturn this tyranny; then if we of the South cried out fraud, intimidation, and unceasingly denounced them for not being thus governed; if we even told the Chinese that they should arm themselves and resist to death any attempt to keep them from ruling, for they had a right to rule, because, forsooth, there were more almond eyes in New England than any other kind of eyes; if we demanded that these Chinese should be received into hotels and churches and schools, and told the New England people that they were horridly wicked not so to receive them, would not such a message as this be sent to us: "Southern brethren, we need your help; send men, send money, to elevate these degraded Chinese; but let us manage the political and social relations—that is 'a domestic and home-rule question?'"

I do not believe that I have written a word counter to Dr. Haygood's meaning. There are two kinds of "intermeddling." Of the kind that Dr. Haygood writes of we want more; of the other every Southern man wants less.

The Negro problem is not "How to secure the Negro his vote at the next election?" nor "How shall caste be instantaneously destroyed?" but "How can we fit the Negro for citizenship?" "How can we elevate him in intelligence and virtue?" This is so pressing that we invoke aid from every quarter. When the Negro has been qualified by education and character he will secure his rights as naturally as the heir enters into his property on reaching his majority. Social relations will adjust themselves to the satisfaction of all concerned. The key to the whole situation is the elevation of the Negro. When this is done all other problems will be self-solving.

BY JULIUS D. DREHER,

President of Roanoke College, Salem, Va.

To the Editor of the Independent: I have your request for a brief expression of my views on the controversy between Dr. Haygood and Senator Eustis on race antagonism in the South. As it is impossible to discuss a subject of so great public concern within the narrow limits prescribed by your letter I must restrict myself to brief mention of a few of the many points that invite attention.

I heartily agree with the spirit of Dr. Haygood's reply to Senator Eustis. It is useless now to attempt to fix the degree of responsibility of the North and the South for the existence or the continuance of slavery. It is worse than useless to seek help in solving our present perplexing problems by indulging in sectional recrimination, in partisan appeals, or, to quote Dr. Haygood, in "Commonplace Satires on the Inconsistencies of the New England Friends of the Negro." In any serious discussion of the Negro problem it needs first to be admitted that the humane sentiment of the civilized world has been growing more and more uncompromisingly opposed to human slavery anywhere and under any forms whatever, and that consequently the abolition of slavery throughout the world has been from the first only a question of time. The early abolitionists in any country are to be regarded as simply pioneers in the cause of humanity, outspoken apostles of human freedom, heralds of the incoming era of universal brotherhood. If we take this broad view of the general question we shall regard the steps leading to emancipation in our own country and in other lands as so many mile-stones on the ample highway of human progress. It helps us little indeed in solving the problems growing out of this great step in our national life to be told that some Northern people have been unwise, inconsistent, and even fanatical on this Negro question. When two school-boys fight, if each finds fault with the other and with his ancestors for generations, that does not settle—it rather aggravates—their little difficulty. If the South blames the North and the North the South, that may all be perfectly natural, and the battle of words may be thick and interminable, since much may easily be said on both sides of the question; but would it not be wiser to leave these old matters of controversy to the impartial verdict of the historian in the distant future and address ourselves to the momentous task of discharging the obligations imposed upon us by the present condition of affairs?

The humane sentiment of the world has doomed slavery, as an institution of modern society; and now the benevolent spirit of the age pronounces against any organized repression of the natural or acquired rights of any class of persons. It recognizes as a maxim that where the need is greatest the call of duty is strongest. This spirit is most active where individual freedom is least restricted, where equality of opportunity exists, and where the highest estimate is placed on man as man. Its aim is to give the greatest happiness to the greatest number, an equal chance to all men to rise, and every wise help and encouragement in the race of life; and all this without regard to nationality, creed, race, color, or condition. It is quite natural that this spirit should seek to protect and elevate the Indian in the West and to educate the Negro in the South and fit him for the duties of manhood and citizenship. The education of the Negro is not simply a Christian, but also a patriotic duty; it is a national problem, a national necessity; and it is a task that cannot be accomplished by the Southern people alone. We ought not, therefore, to consider the benevolent and patriotic efforts of Northern people to aid in this work as intermeddling with the affairs of the South. It would be strange indeed if the Northern people, who are largely responsible for bringing about the emancipation and enfranchisement of the Negro, should not recognize their obligation to aid in fitting him for his new position. Fortunately they not only recognize this duty, but they have the ability and willingness to aid in the solution of this grave problem. According to the census of 1880 New England, with one fourth the population and one twelfth the area of the thirteen Southern States (not including Missouri), had an assessed valuation of property greater than that of the South; and the six Middle States (including Maryland and the District of Columbia), with nearly three fourths the population and not quite one eighth the area had an assessed valuation more than double that of the Southern States. Or, to give the figures: The New England and Middle States combined, area, 182,995 square miles; population, 15,766,582; assessed valuation, $8,216,134,370; the Southern States, area, 818,065 square miles; population, 16,257,393; assessed valuation, $2,370,923,269. A little study of these figures will show how difficult the educational problem is in the South and how easy it is in the North.

In proportion to assessed valuation the South is doing as much as the North for public schools, in appropriations for which the Negroes share equally with the whites. With a taxable basis of $1,584,756,802 (in 1880) Massachusetts finds it an easy matter to keep her common schools open for ten months in a year; while Virginia, with an area more than five times as large and a taxable basis of only $308,455,135, finds it no easy task to keep her schools in session five months of the year. Connecticut, although less than one eighth the area of Kentucky, has nearly as large a taxable basis as that State; while Rhode Island, one forty-seventh the area of Georgia, more than equaled the latter in wealth (in 1880). The Southern people have done nobly in this work of educating both races; but let them do their utmost, and there will still be an ample field inviting the largest private munificence, or—if you please—national bounty. Let us of the South be grateful, then, for Peabody and Slater and hosts of other contributors, and let us not mistake their patriotic gifts to education as intermeddling with the "local" affairs of the South.

With so inadequate provision for public schools we should not be impatient of results in the education of the Negro. So recently in slavery, and still more or less enslaved by the vices incident to that system, the Negro must be tried for several generations before an adequate test can be made of the power of education to elevate him. On the whole he has made steady, if not rapid progress; on the whole he has conducted himself creditably since, as he did during, the War. He is naturally docile and peaceable, and if we treat him with any thing like the fairness, justice, and consideration we claim for ourselves as men we shall hear less of race antagonism in the future. Knowing the peaceable disposition of the Negroes as we do, is it not strange how often the specter of a "Negro uprising" or "Negro riot" is conjured up by heated imaginations and published throughout the Union as an imminent danger to the white race? For myself—Southern man as I am by birth, education and residence—I confess to no little impatience when I read such reports about a race which exhibited so much peaceableness and trustworthiness during the War, and which, unless needlessly provoked or deceived, may be relied upon for a continued exhibition of virtues that are characteristic of the race. The admitted superiority of our race, of which we boast so proudly, imposes upon us the greater obligation to help the colored man to make the most he can out of himself and his situation. This policy of helpfulness and encouragement toward the Negro will do more than any system of repression to promote harmony between the races in the South. And this, it seems to me, does not necessarily mean Negro rule in any Southern State.

New York Independent, February 2, 1889

BY HON. SETH LOW,

Brooklyn, N.Y.[1]

The article of Senator Eustis, of Louisiana, in the October *Forum* of 1888, upon Race Antagonism in the South, and the reply by the Rev. Atticus G. Haygood, are worthy of the most careful attention on the part of thoughtful men both at the North and at the South. Whatever views one may hold upon the subject, it is impossible to read the two papers here discussed without gaining a new and solemn sense of the magnitude and importance of the questions involved in the Negro problem. Senator Eustis labors to establish two propositions. First, that there is a race antagonism between the white man and the Negro which is invincible, and which can be satisfied only by a relation which leaves the Negro in a position distinctly and permanently inferior to the position of the white race. Second, that the solution of the immensely difficult problem involved in this relationship is a question local to the South, and which the South should be permitted to solve in its own way. The second of these propositions Dr. Haygood, one must think, demolishes completely. Neither the Northern conscience nor the Northern intelligence can assume, for one moment, that the rest of the Nation is unconcerned in the solution of this question which is to be reached at the South. Whatever may be the exact nature of the problem, the North is as vitally, if not as immediately, interested in its proper solution as is South Carolina itself.

The first proposition, therefore, that there is a race antagonism which necessitates the relation of inferiors on the part of the Negro race, seems to present the real question for discussion, so far as the settlement of the question is to be advanced by argument. Dr. Haygood frankly takes issue with this proposition, and freely admits that from this stand-point the Senator's conclusions can be understood. It is an advantage that should be made clear

---

[1]Mr. Low's statement of the case did not appear in the Independent with the foregoing contributions to the "Symposium"; it was printed with them in a circular pamphlet by the "Open Letter Club."   A.G.H.

to the Northern mind that a view so radical is seriously entertained by an influential body of opinion in the Southern States. Without argument, and without any serious reflection upon the subject, the practical attitude of the North to the colored population living in their midst would seem to be that before the law the colored man is entitled to the same rights as the white man; that, in the exercise of his right of suffrage, the colored man's ballot is to be as free and as sacred as the ballot of the white man. When the question leaves the domain of public rights society leaves the social relations of the two races to settle themselves. In other words, in the actual conditions prevailing at the North it seems to be clear that the two races can live together upon an equality as to public rights. This is all that is asked should be done in the South. No thoughtful man will dispute that the situation becomes infinitely more embarrassing where the Negroes are in a majority, or even where they represent an important minority. It seems, however, as though these difficulties were not so much incidents of the difference in race as the low standard of development on the part of the Negro in those sections of the country where these conditions prevail. Centuries of slavery and degradation are not to be overcome, even in the uplifting air of America, in a quarter of a century.

To those who look at the matter from a distance Dr. Haygood will seem to be right in his view, that the response on the part of the Negro race to the efforts to educate them, made during the last few years, is sufficiently marked and encouraging to warrant the utmost efforts which can be made along that line, both on the part of the Southern States themselves and of their friends at the North. Meanwhile the one attitude which would seem to make impossible any hopeful progress with the question is precisely that attitude outlined by the Senator, the assumption that a race antagonism exists which will render futile all such efforts. To convince the North that this attitude is correct it will be necessary to break up the Northern conviction that, as matter of fact, it is completely possible for equality of public rights to exist side by side with social relations which adjust themselves unaided by written law. It will further be necessary to demonstrate to the North that a republic can survive, founded upon universal suffrage, in which millions of citizens are compelled to hold a civil position concededly inferior to the position of a great bulk of their countrymen. The question as it presents itself to the Southern mind appears to be, in the words of Senator Morgan, "Shall Negro majorities rule?" The North is unable to appreciate why the South should find itself shut up to this question, except for the fallacy, as it seems to us, which underlies the position taken by Senator Eustis. At the North the Negro vote divides, as well as the white vote. Why is it not possible that both votes should divide at the South, as well as at the North?

Politics aside, there is unquestionably, in all thoughtful circles at the North, the profoundest sympathy for our Southern brothers in the presence of the great problem which lies so close to them, and which yet concerns us only less vitally than it concerns them. This sympathy on the part of many has been outspoken; those who have spoken are but few compared with the great multitude who sincerely cherish this feeling. But even to these, if I may speak as one of them, it seems as though Senator Eustis confuses the issue, and misses the only line along which a solution consistent with republican government upon this continent can by any possibility be found. It seems to such men that the first action which the situation calls for in the South is a change of aim on the part of those whose position enables them to form public sentiment. Instead of aiming to find a *modus vivendi*, in the midst of republican institutions, for an inferior race side by side with a superior race, the aim should be so to divide the votes of both races along the questions of present concern as to make the government of a Southern community a government representative of all its elements instead of only one. Time and education and patience are no doubt necessary for progress along this line as along any other, but the advantage that this has over the attitude taken by Senator Eustis is that the aim, at least, is consistent with the whole basis of popular government as illustrated in the United States. The other aim, which would preserve the domination of the white race, with or without law, is not consistent with a republican form of government. Politicians at the North are likely to find it an unfailing weapon in their hands, as long as it remains the evident policy of the Southern States.

21

THE SOUTHERN CHURCH AND THE NEGRO

(April number (1889) "Cumberland Presbyterian Review.")

For African slavery in the United States, from the beginning of
it to the end of it the only people in this country not in any way
responsible for it were the slaves themselves. They were in America without their seeking, and in slavery against their will. As
a class they took as little part in their emancipation as they did
in their enslavement. No people in slavery ever bore themselves
more patiently, as no people, during a great war that involved
their freedom, ever behaved more magnanimously. It is also true
that no people while in slavery, and by its tuition, ever made such
advances from savagery toward civilization.

Slavery came to its death by the will of God as surely as it
was overruled by Providence to bring many and priceless blessings to the slaves themselves. He is a poor student of the ways of
God with men who, in his abhorrence of any of the ways of men,
closes his eyes to the facts of Providential history. Dr. Mayo, of
Boston, in an address at Ocean Grove, N.J., in 1883, stated a
great and indisputable fact when he said that although, under
the old *regime,* the slaves were shut out from the opportunities
of book learning. "American slavery itself was perhaps the most
effective university through which any race of savages was ever
introduced into civilization."

During slavery and through slavery the Negroes in America
made more progress in the arts and training of Christian civili-

zation than all their ancestors ever made, than all their kindred in Africa have made. They learned how to make crops, and, on the side of material life, this is the first step out of barbarism. They learned the English language well enough to receive, while in slavery, many of the best lessons Christian people could teach them and to begin their education in books the day they were made free. On this foundation has been laid the educational work among these people since 1865. What they learned before 1865 made it possible for the facts of 1889 to exist; in 1889 two millions of them can at least read the word of God, and more than one million of them are at school.

While in slavery the Negro learned much in many directions. While not ready for citizenship when its perils and responsibilities were suddenly laid upon him, he had, while a slave, learned more of law and civil order than all the Negroes in Africa know, and it was what he had learned that made his citizenship, when he emerged from slavery, possible to him or at all possible to others. Best of all things, he had learned much of the Christian religion. In 1865 a half million of them were in the communion of the Christian Churches of the South; all of them knew much of Christianity, and all of them were, to a degree, under its benign influence.

These statements are not made in defense of slavery—in a world that belongs to Jesus Christ slavery is not defensible—but in recognition of unmistakable facts that cannot be ignored, if we would reach any rational and Christian conclusions concerning these strange people whose fortunes are inextricably joined with the fortunes of the white people of this country.

Seeing that the most important fact in the history of the African people in this country has been the Christianizing of hundreds of thousands of them, no Christian thinker can doubt that Christianizing them was God's design in their coming to this country. It is equally clear as to the duty of Christian people concerning the Negro race in our midst—whether we think of to-day or to-morrow—that we must determine all things from the Christian stand-point. Economic, political, and social questions necessarily grow out of the facts of this problem, but its true solution is forever and utterly impossible except upon the platform of the Gospel of the Son of God. It pleased God to select the Southern rather than the Northern States of the Union as the chosen field for working out this stupendous race problem that involves the destiny of two continents. The divine election did not turn upon accident; it was determined in unfailing wisdom. This burden God laid upon the Southern people because they were fittest to bear it and perform the duties that grew out of their relations to the Negro race. Thousands of them failed in their duty to God and to their lowly brother, but thousands of them did not fail. They did better than any other people in their case would have done; else the problem committed to them would have been laid upon others who, in God's prevision, would have done better with it.

Some reasons that entered into the selection of the South and of its people, as best suited to forward the stupendous schemes of Providence, seem very plain; others, equally important, we may never know. For one thing, these African children in the school of Providence needed a warm but not an enervating climate. That the Southern States suited the physical conditions of the problem is evidenced in the improved breed of men of African descent that exists among us to-day. Neither in climate nor other conditions were the New England or other Northern States adapted to his physical or other wants. The Negroes in this preparatory school, through which Providence conducted them, needed the protection and guidance of a stronger people, devoted chiefly to agriculture, and yet of a people who would be patient with their pupils. To whatever it may be attributed, it is certain that the white people of the South, both before and since 1865, in their personal relations with Negroes are more patient with them than any other white people who have ever had dealings with them. It is a matter of moment, in the consideration of this question, that this stronger race—outside of Louisiana, where slavery was at its worst—was homogeneous in blood and Protestant in religion. Many failures in duty and many grievous wrongs history justly writes against the master class. None of these will a candid man seek to defend or explain away. But it will help candid people, who were not chosen to bear this burden, to judge the South fairly to consider a few things that many seem never to have known. 1. The Southern people did better for their slaves than any other people ever did for slaves. The history that tells of slavery in New England will not furnish contradiction to this statement. 2. Southern masters are not alone in dealing hardly with dependents. This does not excuse any who failed or sinned, but it suggests a reason why those who would cast the stones of judgment should consider our Lord's words to those who were eager to punish the young girl taken in sin. 3. This also is true: wherein any have sinned all have suffered. For every wrong done to defenseless slaves the whole race of masters paid a penalty, of which the loss in money values is so small a part that it is not worth considering.

How God overruled slavery and brought out of it great blessings to the African people under its yoke is illustrated in the marvelous progress of these people since slavery came to its death. On the foundations laid before 1865 Christian philanthropy and enlightened public policy have built a work absolutely matchless in history. When the Revolution, so far as actual war is concerned, ended at Appomattox, nearly five millions who had been slaves were made free in law and in fact. Presently they were citizens and voters. No people ever confronted a greater or more imminent peril. Whether the trial of what virtues may exist in human nature was harder in its pressure upon the late masters or the late slaves God only knows. Nothing in the previous habits or education of either class prepared them for the new conditions that came in a day. One class did not know the rights, the other did not know the duties, of free labor. And herein is the explanation of most of the troubles and irritations that have vexed the South so long.

The Southern white people, who for generations had been the only teachers the Negroes had ever had, were, for the time at least, disqualified for carrying on their education under the new conditions that came with the emancipation of both races from slavery. They were broken in fortune and could not establish and conduct colleges and training-schools for the Negroes—they could not then educate their own children. They were disqualified also by the results in them—in their habits, thoughts, and sentiments—of their relations to the Negroes both as slaves and freedmen. These personal disqualifications were natural to their position; it could not have been otherwise. It cannot be proved that any other people, similarly placed, would have thought and felt otherwise than the Southern white people thought and felt, for no other people were ever similarly placed. Whether, as to all these difficult matters, the Southern people have labored well or ill, this is certain: there is nothing in history to furnish a basis of comparison. This history stands alone. If there were to be colleges and other higher schools for Negro youth for some years after emancipation it is certain that other than Southern white people had to establish them. Southern white people could not had they been minded to do it; had they been able they would not have done it.

The Northern people came out of the war richer than they entered it. For this Southern people, white and black, should give thanks; had the North in 1865 been as poor as the South was the end would have come. In the mercy of God toward these five million of poor Negroes, and to their white neighbors as well (for the right education of the black man in the South is nearly as important to the white man as to his dark brother), the people who had money had inclination. Zeal and cash for once came together.

Having studied this subject for many years, and with opportunities to know the facts beyond what most people have had, I wish to say, Never in the history of Christian benevolence and Christian endeavor was a great and emergent duty more nobly met than was the duty of trying to prepare the freedmen for freedom met by Christian men and women of the Northern States.

The most ardent eulogist of the good men and women who gave themselves with heroic abandon and Christian consecration to this wide and hard field of missionary service will, if he knows the facts and is of candid temper, admit that among them were not a few who were unfitted for a work as delicate as it was difficult. Among the wise were "cranks"; among the unselfish were some who had private ends to serve; among the zealous some who were "busybodies" in matters that did not concern their mission. These "difficult people" did unspeakable harm to the cause they unwisely and unworthily championed. Concerning these matters I do not guess; I have had observation and personal knowledge. But it should surprise no student of Christian history; it has always been so. Good people have always suffered misjudgments because bad people have professed adherence to their cause; wise people have been confounded because foolish people brought reproach upon them. But it would be as just to hold St. Paul responsible for Simon Magus as to charge upon the wise and good men and women, who came out of Christian homes in the North to teach in Negro schools, the follies and sins of those unworthy ones who should never have entered this field at all.

The flippant sneer of certain ill-informed or very wicked Southern people, that these teachers came South because they could get no employment North, that the small pay they have received measures the motive of their zeal, is as base and unjust a slander as was ever invented by malignant prejudice since slander was first used against the good and pure. It were as just to denounce citizenship because some men sell their votes; to throw foreign missions overboard because an occasional lunatic or impostor is employed by a mistaken Board of Managers; to repudiate gold because there are counterfeits; to forsake the Church of God because some hypocrites have made " gain of godliness."

Hundreds of the men and women engaged in the work of teaching Negro colleges and other training-schools it has been my privilege to know, to honor, and to love. The foremost colleges and universities and Churches in the North have their representatives in this work. Nobler people than many of them I have never known; of better people I have never read. Those who scorn them can have but one excuse—ignorance. But where there has been opportunity to know the truth, ignorance is not an excuse one will stand by in the presence of the King.

The history of this work of educating the emancipated people once more and in a very noble way illustrates that saying of our Lord, "Wisdom is justified of her children." The work of the past twenty-three years has been costly—in money, the least, and in lives, the highest of all values. Millions of dollars have gone into the work of the colleges and other great training-schools, and several thousands of precious lives whose worth cannot be estimated by any measures of value known to this world. But the good done is worth more than it all cost—all the money, all the hard work, all the isolation and ostracism and pain of heart. Many of these good men and women have entered deeply into the fellowship of His sufferings, of whom the prophet says, "He shall see of the travail of his soul and be satisfied."

The great facts that lie on the surface and that can be put into figures challenge not only respect, but wonder. If it be true that no poor and destitute people ever received so much help in any twenty-three years, it is also true that no illiterate people ever made so great progress in learning in the same period.

This vast educational work is distinctly Christian. The great schools are conducted by Christian men and women; in all of them the Bible holds the place of honor. In all of them the aim is to build up men and women in the virtues that constitute Christian character. Revivals of religion are as common and as thorough in these Negro colleges as in any Christian colleges for white youth in any Christian country.

The work shows for itself; it has been well done; the fruit of this tree is good. The best and most useful members of the African race in the Southern States are the men and women who have had Christian education in these schools. In them are not only the best progressive forces at work among these people, but also the best conservative influences. In these men and women we have the best guarantee of the advancement of the African race in our country and the best assurance of social and civil order that they can give.

The school-work done by these Northern missionaries is by no means the only work that they have done. They have done nearly all the evangelistic work that white people have done among the Negroes since 1865. The Southern Churches did a good, great, and abiding work under the old conditions. The Northern Churches have done nearly all since the new conditions obtained that the Negroes have not done for themselves. This is also true: Those Negroes who have done the best work in teaching and preaching among their own people have been trained and made what they are in the institutions conducted by white men and women from the North. Nearly all the money and nearly all the personal service has been Northern.

But has the Southern Church no duty to perform, no work to do for these millions of black people, not in Africa, speaking languages unknown to us, but here in our midst, brought up with us, speaking our own English tongue; our neighbors, our fellow-citizens, and our brothers? More and more this question presses itself upon us. We cannot put it away; every day it will come back to us till we answer it aright—answer it as Jesus Christ would have us answer.

It is a great and singular mistake of many excellent Northern people, when they conclude that Southern white people have done next to nothing for the education of the Negro. The Southern white people, so far as the payment of money goes, have done far more than all outsiders together. It is a misfortune that many Northern people, with the best intentions, it may be, but with a very misleading pre-conception, reach their conclusions on this subject by a process of logic rather than by an investigation of facts. If there were no figures upon the subject the conclusion is upon the surface that the Southern white people have borne and are now bearing, and will continue to bear, the chief burden of educating the Negro race in the Southern States. The proof is easy and complete; it costs vastly more to maintain the sixteen thousand public schools, attended by more than one million Negro children, than to conduct the colleges and universities in which their teachers are trained. That the white people pay nearly all the taxes is conceded; one of the best statisticians estimates that the white people of the South pay ninety-one dollars out of every hundred dollars of the taxes.

Take two illustrations where each Southern State might testify. From 1871 to 1888 Virginia expended $3,709,500 upon public schools for Negro youth; upon normal and collegiate institutions, for the higher education of Negroes, $247,000. During the same period Alabama expended on public schools for Negro youth $3,296,793.24; upon normal schools for the Negroes, $107,500. Similar statements might be made for other Southern States; these are used here simply because the reports for Virginia and Alabama were on my desk when this article was being written. All the Churches and societies have not expended such sums, or any thing like such sums, in Virginia and Alabama. They could not; only Government could expend such sums in the education of the masses. These States, and the other Southern States, would have used true economy, and would have observed sound public policy had they spent a great deal more than they have invested in the education of the people, but just history will say that they have done more in preparing the Negro for citizenship than all the world has done. Not counting Maryland, West Virginia, or Missouri, the Southern States have invested in the education of the Negro since 1868 *more than thirty-seven millions of dollars.*

But the work done by the State school systems and, therefore, by the people, whose money supports them, cannot put out of discussion the question before us: "What is the duty of the Southern Church to the Negro citizen, neighbor, and brother?" Christian people must consider this question, not to find a philosophy of it, or to vindicate a theory of it, but to ascertain a duty and find the best way for discharging it. If other people were able and willing to do all for the Christian elevation of the Negro that he needs, if other people were actually to do these necessary things, Southern Christians would not thereby be exempt from duties of their own. Duties grow out of relations and opportunities. If a hungry man be near me my duty is not performed when another afar off feeds him. In such a case if the hungry man needs nothing from me I need something from him. It is ruin to me to dehumanize myself in failing to relieve the hunger at my door. It ought to be true that Southern white people can, better than any other white people, help the Negro to become what he ought to be. If this be true we are under an obligation that no sort of reasoning can explain away and that no sort of prejudice can weaken.

It is a common belief among Southern people that they understand the Negro and his peculiarities more perfectly than any other people can understand him. Indeed, not a few Southern white people think that they know, the Negro better than he knows himself. This maybe so; self-knowledge is not more readily acquired by a whole race than by an individual member of it. The Southern white people should understand the Negro better than other people; their opportunity for knowing him has been best. On one point my observation leads me to doubt; it is not clear to me that the average Southern white man knows the free Negro—especially the educated Negro—as well as he knew him as a slave. But it is certain that the Southern white man's knowledge of the Negro is good enough to lay upon him an obligation he cannot escape—that, if he have the Spirit of Christ in him, he will not desire to escape: an obligation to help the Negro to become in fact as well as in law a Christian citizen and a Christian man of as high order as his gifts and opportunities allow. It is clear to the common sense of the case that Southern white Christians can, if they will, do much good to the Negro that no others can do. But if it were otherwise they must do part of this work. If it be "more blessed to give than to receive," the Southern white people cannot afford to stand idly by and see others do their work for them. It may be that we need the good that would come to us from helping the Negro more than the Negro needs what we can do for him.

I do not wish at this time to make the argument on a lower plane than that of Christian duty; but it is well worth the attention of the wise whether the let-alone policy is sound public policy for the Southern people. If we have views of government and civil order that are good; if we have ways of living that are commendable; if we have sentiments that are worthy, is it wise in us to leave the training of the future leaders of the Negro race in our midst to other people, with other views and ways and sentiments?

Concluding this article, I suggest the most important and altogether helpful things that Southern white Christians can at this time do for the cause of the Christian uplifting of the Negro race:

1. By every token the first duty we owe the Negro is to study his case with absolute fairness. If his education be the special topic under consideration, find out the facts. They are accessible, and good people who are wise will not ignore them.

2. The second duty most important at this time, the thing that will be most helpful, next to finding out the facts, is simply this: To treat courteously, kindly, and justly, the good men and women who are trying to do for the Negro what we have not done—educate him. This we can all do; this we will do if we walk in the light that Jesus Christ has given to us. If we do as he would do in our place—and, therefore, as he would have us do—this much, and it is a very great deal, we can do to help the cause of the Christian education of the Negro: we can forever have done with the social ostracism of God's servants who are teaching the ignorant how to read—who are training the untrained to be Christian men and women.

When we study the case, when we know the facts, and deal in a Christian spirit by those who are working to do the Negro good, then we will be ready to begin work ourselves.

ALSO FROM DEWARD PUBLISHING:

The Man of Galilee
Atticus G. Haygood

Dr. Haygood's apologetic for the deity of Christ using Jesus Himself as presented by the gospel records as its chief evidence. This is a reprint of the 1963 edition. The Man of Galilee was originally published in 1889. 108 pages. $8.99.

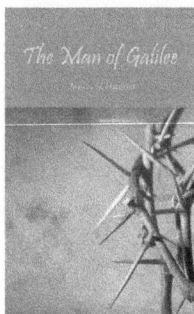

Beneath the Cross: Essays and Reflections on the Lord's Supper
Jady S. Copeland and Nathan Ward (editors)

The Lord's Supper is rich with meaning supplied by Old Testament foreshadowing and New Testament teaching. Explore the depths of symbolism and meaning found in the last hours of the Lord's life in *Beneath the Cross*. Filled with short essays by preachers, scholars, and other Christians, this book is an excellent tool for preparing meaningful Lord's Supper thoughts—or simply for personal study and meditation. 329 pages. $14.99 (PB); $23.99 (HB).

Boot Camp: Equipping Men with Integrity for Spiritual Warfare
Jason Hardin

According to Steve Arterburn, best-selling author of *Every Man's Battle,* "This is a great book to help us men live opposite of this world's model of man."

Boot Camp is the first volume in the IMAGE series of books for men. It serves as a Basic Training manual in the spiritual war for honor, integrity and a God-glorifying life. 237 pages, $13.99 (PB); $24.99 (HB).

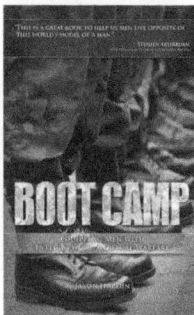

Invitation to a Spiritual Revolution
Paul Earnhart
Few preachers have studied the Sermon on the Mount as intensively or spoken on its contents so frequently and effectively as the author of this work. His excellent and very readable written analysis appeared first as a series of articles in *Christianity Magazine*. By popular demand it is here offered in one volume so that it can be more easily preserved, circulated, read, reread and made available to those who would not otherwise have access to it. 173 pages. $10.99.

The Growth of the Seed: Notes on the Book of Genesis
Nathan Ward
A study of the book of Genesis that emphasizes two primary themes: the development of the Messianic line and the growing enmity between the righteous and the wicked. In addition, it provides detailed comments on the text and short essays on several subjects that are suggested in, yet peripheral to, Genesis. 537 pages. $19.99.

Churches of the New Testament
Ethan R. Longhenry
A study designed to investigate every local congregation concerning which the Bible provides some information: it considers the geography and history of each city, whatever is known about the beginnings of the church in the city, and an analysis of the church based upon what is revealed in the New Testament. 150 pages. $9.99.

The Big Picture of the Bible
Kenneth W. Craig
In this short book, the author summarizes the central theme of the Bible in a simple, yet comprehensive approach. Evangelists across the world have used this presentation to convert countless souls to the discipleship of Jesus Christ. Bulk discounts will be available, as will special pricing for congregational orders. 48 pages, color. $4.99.

From Gravel to Glory: Becoming a House of God
Gina Calvert
Drawing on her studies of the tabernacle and temple, Calvert digs deeply into her own difficult spiritual journey to demonstrate how every experience we have is related to being a house of God. With surprising candor, Calvert takes us from our origins as "a pile of rocks and a promise" to a glorious temple. 185 pages. $12.99.

For a full listing of our titles, visit our website: www.dewardpublishing.com

DEWARD
PUBLISHING COMPANY

www.ingramcontent.com/pod-product-compliance
Lightning Source LLC
Chambersburg PA
CBHW030006290326
41934CB00005B/249